# MORE PRAISE FOR
## A RENAISSANCE REDNECK IN A
## MEGA-CHURCH PULPIT

"When a book makes you laugh out loud, it is a winner. When it makes you cry, it is a truth-teller. But when it changes you, it becomes a wise friend. Randy Elrod has managed all three of these in *A Renaissance Redneck in a Mega-Church Pulpit*."

**–Margaret Becker**, Award-winning Singer/Songwriter and Author

"This book brings out every emotion I've ever experienced, and a couple I didn't know I was capable of expressing. The raw, yet tender transparency; the blunt, yet sensitive perspectives; the ugly, yet beautiful insights all blend together in the life of one who has been blessed, bombarded, and is boldly acknowledging God's hand at work in all of it.

Every pastor should read this before hiring the next staff member. It might help to see how a creative perceives reality; it just might help the pastors to see themselves more clearly, also!"

**–Rev. L. C. Campbell, Jr.**, Founding Pastor, Nettles Island Church, Stuart, FL, and formerly of Church #2 of this book

*Please turn the page*
*for more reviews. . . .*

"Life wounds all of us. We patch those wounds with the wrong things and lose ourselves.

This is the painful, messy, and beautiful story of how one man sheds the skin of his false self in order to find his true one.

Most people never do that, for it requires much courage and good guides.

**–Lucille Zimmerman**, Licensed Professional Counselor and Author of *Renewed: Finding Your Inner Happy in an Overwhelmed World*

"In the opening chapters of this book, Randy Elrod frames a world so unfamiliar to most that it would seem incredible to the reader if not held together by such personal vulnerability.

Imagine Lake Wobegon meets *Duck Dynasty*. Colorful characters and recalled with the humor and poetry of Garrison Keillor while the setting of Randy's childhood, the Tennessee Appalachian foothills, would be perfect fodder for A&E's next unbelievable 'reality' show."

**–Jonathan Ford**, Pastor of Worship & Arts, King Street Church, Chambersburg, PA

6/14

Keith,

Thanks for your friendship

Ann ENCOURAGEMENT!.

ALSO BY

# RANDY ELROD

SEX, LIES & RELIGION

BEAUTY IS CALLING

LETTERS FROM A DEVASTATED ARTIST

# A RENAISSANCE REDNECK IN A MEGA-CHURCH PULPIT

RANDY ELROD

# CONTACT RANDY

## To book Randy for speaking:
createconference@gmail.com

## For more information:
www.renaissanceredneck.com

Library of Congress Control Number: 2010900033
Printed in the United States of America
ISBN # 978-0-991-47150-8

cre:ate 2.0
Publishing

# DEDICATION

To Dr. Steve
A wise guide.

# CONTENTS

## PART I
## THE REDNECK YEARS

## PART II
## THE MEGA-CHURCH YEARS

## PART III
## THE RENAISSANCE YEARS

# PART 1
# THE REDNECK YEARS

# CHAPTER 1

# A FORESHADOWING

I am a Southerner. I was born in Chattanooga, in the volunteer state of Tennessee, and grew up in the privation of the Appalachian foothills. So I am a Southerner of Southerners—and redneck; and for many years, was nearly barren of culture, I suppose—or invigoration, if you will.

My father worked third shift at a yarn mill down the mountain, and on Sundays he was an itinerant preacher and musician. In the daytime he worked odd jobs like tearing old houses down and helping my grandpa, who was a stonemason. He didn't sleep very much.

1

When I reached the ripe 'ole age of twelve, he brought me a white bag that could have swallowed me whole. It had *News-Free Press* printed on the side in big red letters, a wide shoulder strap, and smelled of cotton and print. Dad told me it was time to get to working. He explained the best way for a boy like me to get some business knowledge was by throwing newspapers.

It was time I started earning my keep, so from now on, I would be buying all my clothes and personal items. That was the beginning of what I later learned was my entrepreneurial pursuits.

I quickly realized this did not exclude me from my household chores. This included the dreaded getting up cold at dark-thirty before everyone else, and fetching Appalachian fuel from the icy coal pile in the backyard. I would then light and stoke our old cast-iron stove until it was so hot it glowed an eerie transparent red-orange, emitting odors of oil and sulfur—smells our mining community called money.

There were other chores including hoeing the endless rows of corn and potatoes in the garden. That job was to be done first thing after getting off the bus from school. Every Saturday I would use that same garden hoe and a rusty wheelbarrow to mix sand, water, and cement into mortar for my grandpa.

Two fast years later, as a man-child of fourteen, Mom drove me to a government building to get my work permit. This allowed me to go down the mountain to a drive-in hamburger joint and learn a real trade; learn all there was to it; learn to make people happy: young, old, long hairs, short hairs, gray hairs—all sorts of uniquely made humankind.

Why, I could make anybody happy! Anybody in the world; it didn't make no difference who. And if there wasn't any quick new-fangled way to satisfy a customer, I could invent one—and do it as easy as rolling off a log.

I soon became head cashier at the original Burger King. To be totally honest, there could only be one cashier at a time—it was a very small eating establishment—but I was it, and I loved making people happy because then they liked me.

Well a boy like me is full of ambition—that goes without saying. With eager customers hungry all hours of a day, all days of a year, and all years of a life, one gets plenty of practice making people happy. I did anyway.

But one day I met my match and I got my dose. And that's really what this book is all about.

To fully explain it, I have to go back to those damn preaching and singing genes I picked up from my father, and from his father, and from my mom's father, and probably from their fathers too.

Those genes were the ones I didn't get to choose and buy with my earnings (like the jeans I have on now), but I nonetheless wore them, and they kept me completely covered up for the first forty or so years of my life.

Making people happy proved to be a big job. Much bigger than I ever dreamed. But I kept right on doing it because I liked how it made me feel. It was my calling, you see—my purpose in life.

And that calling—that destiny—eventually plucked me right out of the poverty and illiteracy of the Appalachians, and deposited me into some of the wealthiest and most artistic places the world has ever known.

But wait; I'm getting ahead of the story.

3

# CHAPTER 2

## MY EARLY YEARS

Dad was seventeen when I became a gleam in his eye. The pretty young bride with dark curly tresses, seven days his younger, who returned that gleam is the lady I call Mom. He still lovingly calls her wife after almost sixty years.

In the mountains of Tennessee, it's okay for children to have children. In fact, it's expected. If a woman gets to be eighteen and is not married, she is practically given up as an old maid. So as could be expected, my brother and sister appeared soon after me, before Mom and Dad were of legal drinking age.

5

We moved around a lot. I attended thirteen schools in four different states. We would try out an adjoining state for a few months, but somehow always ended up back in Tennessee. I changed teachers and friends like some people change clothes. Maybe that's what has always put me at ease about meeting new people—'cause I knew so dad-blamed many of them.

My mom says she doesn't think I ever met a stranger. Of course, since shyness runs in the rest of the family, she also says that sometimes she can't believe she birthed me. What gives me some measure of security is that all our lives (which, if you do your math, adds up to almost the same number), we have practically looked like twins. With all my other insecurities, the last thing I needed was to go looking around the mountains for my birth mother.

My first recollection of a real home was the one with the eerie coal stove. While some people lovingly recount their entire lives spent at one old home place, we Elrods measured time lived in homes not in days, nor years, but in minutes. And since even a few minutes spent in this house were more than enough, that might have been a good thing.

Before Dad began building on, we had three rooms. There was a small kitchen with a very rambunctious wringer washer that would suddenly rattle and shake around like the holy rollers at our church on Sunday. There was a tiny four-by-four-foot hallway in the center, where the stove was; and a tiny bathroom with a window and no screen that looked out onto the sandy and worn battleground I used for my little green army men. We kids were really proud of that indoor bathroom, because in a previous house, the water would always freeze, and the only alternative was the dilapidated outhouse.

We all shared a bedroom where my sister once swallowed a penny during the night and caused quite a stir. She slept in a squeaky cot in the middle of the room, and my brother and I in bunk beds Mom got from Goodwill. We were placed against the inside wall, and our parents had a bed, catty-cornered on the outside wall.

6

There was also a modest living room with a Naugahyde sofa, which was supposed to be a great new invention that looked like leather, but instead it just looked, felt, and smelled like rubber. If you tried to take a nap on it, you would get all hot and sweaty. We also had an ancient upright piano with worn-down keys and a foot pedal that squeaked.

We had a table in the kitchen, similar to one you would find in a '50s diner, and we were able to eat there when the wringer washer was taking a rest. The living room was where, under duress, I took piano lessons from Ezra Knight. The duress part was because even though I loved music, it seemed every dad-gone lesson was at the exact same time my friends were playing ball and generally having fun just outside the door and down the cement block steps. That door, I might add, was always open because we did not (nor did anyone else) have air conditioning.

The bedroom was always off limits to us kids on Sunday afternoons 'cause Mom and Dad would need a "nap." It wasn't until the sixth (yes, sixth) grade that I found out it had been one of those mysterious "naps" that begot me, not just the fervent prayers for a child that this ever-questioning boy had originally been led to believe by my parents.

It happened this way. A toughie named Sam pulled out his wiener in front of Suzie in the back of the bus and said, "Wanna make a baby?" And preacher-boy me blurted out, "That's not how my mom and dad made *me*. They asked God for a boy, and God, in His goodness, granted their prayer." It was like lightning struck the bus right then and there. Everyone got really quiet and Sam sheepishly put his little penis back in his jeans.

For some reason, it was me and not Sam who felt his face burning bright red. I slumped down in the seat feeling very alone, and rode home less a child than when the trip began. Imagine my surprise and shock to realize I had not been conceived immaculately to a young groom and bride of seventeen through the miracle of prayer. I really thought I had been blessed to have more in common with Jesus

7

than most folks. Admittedly, I hadn't been conceived of a virgin, but an innocent seventeen-year-old bride like my mom was pretty darn close.

I soon also realized that *unlike* my mom, innocence was a rarified term that very few mountain folk possessed. One fateful day, we drove down into an isolated mountain cove —God knows where—and sat in the sweltry car, picking at each other like bored kids do, as Dad got out and went "visiting" for a while. Now for those of you not familiar with such high-falootin' religious terms, "visiting" is when the preacher goes to a prospective churchgoer's house and gets to know them.

And boy did Dad get to know *these* people. I suspect from his hushed conversation with Mom later (which I just happened to overhear), he found out more than he bargained for.

Dad finally came back after what seemed like days, but was actually about an hour, and he was toting "tithes." That's another high-falootin' religious term (by the way, you'll see I know lots of them) that means a tenth. In the holy King James Version of the Bible, every family was required to give a tenth of their crops to the Lord. Well, in this case, I gathered that the Lord was my dad, and the tithe was a ragged, greasy brown paper bag stuffed with leftover garden vegetables that he placed in the turtle (you should know that in mountain jargon, a car trunk is called a turtle).

This seems as good a time as any to explain our distinctive way of talking. The isolation of mountain life transformed the English language—words were mispronounced, phrases and sentences were rearranged, and new words were created to fit the rugged mountain life the early settlers faced. As you will see, illiteracy and intermarriage within mountain communities also caused this unique speech to flourish, even to this day.

One can still hear some of the original dialect in the more isolated mountain communities like the one I grew up in. If you find yourself in such places, listen closely for unique words and sayings like: *a-childing* (pregnant),

8

*corn-fed critters* (poor people), *a give-out* (an announcement), *a whoop and a holler* (a long distance), *bald-faced whiskey* (fresh whiskey from a still), *gully-washer* (heavy rain), *death watch* (ticking insect in the wall of a house that meant a death in the family), *dogtrot* (covered passageway between two rooms), *et* (ate), *fur* (far), *you'uns* (ya'll), *pap* (father), *pile up with trash* (to associate with low-class, immoral people), *since Heck was a pup* (a long time ago), and *I'm not bigging it* (exaggerating), either.

That day as we drove home up the steep, hairpin curves of the washboard road with the windows down to get relief from the heat, all you could see and taste was billowing yellow dust. When no one was lookin', my brother Terry and I would spit the grit into the back floorboard of our two-tone '57 Chevy station wagon. We had tried spitting out the window once, but it just flew back in and ran down our faces.

As we listened, we heard Dad relating a story to Mom that could only take place in the Appalachian backwoods of Tennessee. I swear on a stack of Bibles, this story is true.

It seems as Dad was visiting this family and inviting them to church, it somehow came out that the patriarch of the home had lost his wife a few weeks back. Dad was extending his condolences when the man hastened to tell him it was okay, since he had already gotten another one. He said since there were no other available women around those parts, he just went ahead and laid claim to the only female available. It seemed of no apparent consequence to him that this fair maiden happened to be his own granddaughter.

Being a rather precocious child at that time, I innocently asked in my enthusiastic treble twang, "Mom, does that mean she's her own grandma?" It was one of those times when everything got real quiet, and finally Dad started whistling like he did sometimes when there was a void in the air.

There was a boy who lived down the road from our parsonage (that's religious high-falootin' talk for the rundown house the church people give the pastor and his

9

family so they can keep an eye on them). Anyway, that young buck first taught me that a turtle is really called a trunk, and a few other things I can't mention in mixed company—but he had a grandpa who was also worthy of a few words.

His dad was named Boogus and everybody reverently called his grandpa Mr. Hatfield. To add clarification to this story, the better adverb might have been fearfully, rather than reverently. Mr. Hatfield's given name was Cletus, but I never heard anyone call him that. They always used an epithet and it was whispered around that he was related to Mr. William Anse Hatfield of the West Virginia Hatfields. His nickname was Devil—Devil Cletus Hatfield. As you will see, he was appropriately named.

Mr. Hatfield lived down the cove from our church and he would always come in the back door and walk to his pew. And when I say his pew, I really mean it was his pew. No one else ever sat there. Ever. You could hear the cloth of his faded overalls rubbing the pew and the clunk of his cane as he shuffled to the left wall of the church. There was an uneven greasy spot on the drywall where he would take off his hat and lean his head. As he sat down, you could hear the distinct thump of his gun against the pew. Inevitably, he would fall asleep as the service progressed and begin to snore in a surprisingly soft and rhythmic manner.

When Dad finally was received into the community as a favored outsider—and make no mistake, unless you were born and raised there, no matter *how long* you stayed, you were always an outsider—our family learned that we had been granted an audience at Mr. Hatfield's house. It was next to impossible to keep my anxiety and curiosity from eating the heart out of me until it was time to pay that visit.

Mr. Hatfield, with his greasy spot and gun, had always been an enigma to this greenhorn and as yet unarmed (unless you count my cap gun) boy. So I cannot begin to describe the sights, frights, and delights of that visit. But I will certainly try.

When we arrived, Mr. Hatfield, who had not given himself the comfort of a wash, knelt down close and looked

10

me over with a smiling and impudent curiosity. It didn't appear he had ever laid eyes on me 'til that very minute, even though he had passed by me plenty of times at church. His smell nor his consideration fazed me. I told you I ain't never met a stranger, and this was to be no exception.

Our tall but now stooped and wizened host helped settle in my somewhat uneasy mom and dad at the old wooden table, in a kitchen that smelled like rotting paper or dirty socks. The table had one of those red-and-white-checkered tablecloths that always feels like greasy plastic. You could slide your thumb around in circles as easy as can be. My sis, who could not be pried from Mom's side with a crowbar, would not touch it.

Mr. Hatfield offered us what he called grape juice. He told us that he'd made it with his very own grapes from the yard. He called them *musk-ee-dines*. Having never heard that term before, I warily took a sip—and was sold from that very moment. It was mighty tasty. Everybody liked it, even my sis Cheryl, who could be a tad picky at times.

It tasted sweet, sort of like that candy-flavored cough medicine Mom would give us. But the more you drank, the less mediciney it became. It just got better and better. A little later, as we mosied out to the front porch at Mr. Hatfield's invitation to "sip a bit," I noticed my parents starting to relax, almost as if by magic, and my sis kept giggling.

After sitting for a spell and "visiting," Mr. Hatfield asked Mom if it would please her if the menfolk excused ourselves to take a stroll and look around. By that time, my brother Terry and I had sat still long enough. I reckoned we must have been ensconced on the edge of those decomposing wooden steps for what seemed like at least ten years, and as far as I was concerned, that officially qualified us as menfolk.

We proudly sauntered away with the fellows, sure the women folk couldn't help but watch and be a tad bit jealous of our masculine camaraderie. I grabbed a blade of grass, sucked on it, and savored the strange sense of euphoria that seemed to have anointed my every member. Come to think of it, *all* the members of our little soiree seemed to have been struck with a similar euphoric anointing. And we wasn't even at church.

Being hungry for man talk, I turned all my curiosity to the circumstances of this opportunity, and was elated and ready to make the most out of it that could be made. I sidled up beside the shambling Mr. Hatfield like I belonged, pulled myself up as tall as I could, and asked, "Now tell me, honest and true, how long you lived here without electrification?" 'Cause there was nary a power line to be seen down there in the wilds of that isolated domicile.

As I scrutinized his face for an answer, his rheumy but steely gray eyes fixed on me and he chewed thoughtfully on what I knew was certainly *not* a blade of grass. A moist dribble of brown oozed downward through his poorly shaved and graying stubble. It originated from the droopy right-hand corner of his mouth, continued along a misshapen jaw line that I'm sure had once been square enough to chisel granite, and cascaded amidst his pendulous dewlaps, disappearing beneath his stained and faded undershirt.

He, also being euphoric, began to talk in a happy, thoughtless, almost boyish fashion, as we walked along. My dad and brother were quite content to trail behind and let me carry the conversation. We made friends at once. He told me all sorts of things about himself and would ask me an occasional question about myself, but never waited for an answer.

As we strolled and talked, we came up to an old abandoned well. It was round and made of mountain rock and was about three feet tall. It had two round wooden columns supporting an angled roof covered in wood shakes, and still had a tattered rope wrapped around an old dowel. The opening of the well was covered with several crisscrossed layers of old boards and rusty metal.

Standing there filled with euphoria, he recounted a story that still makes the cold chills creep over me. As it goes, he and his former wife got in a fight once, and he got over it and *she* didn't. As he laid accent upon the word *she*, he leered sideways at the well with those steely gray eyes, and as if on cue, I swear it, the scream of a raven echoed eerily through the cove.

We all unconsciously edged away from the well, and like a man who realized he may have said too much, he came to his senses, and said a little too hastily, "I was just joshing. Now, let's go make sure that wife of *yours* is still doing okay, Revh-rand." He pointed back toward the house with a massive but gently shaking hand, pockmarked with blue dots. (I learned later those came from a coal-mining explosion.)

Something in me seemed to believe his story—my consciousness, you could say; but my reason just couldn't. My reason straightway began to clamor and I suppose that was natural. I didn't know how to go about satisfying it, because I knew the normal laws of men didn't apply in these parts. My consciousness screamed he was a murderer, but my budding reason said if the man was sane, he wouldn't be capable of killing his own wife. She probably just took a long trip somewhere, or something like that. At least, that's what I told myself.

It was the first time my consciousness and reason got into a serious tussle. And it wouldn't be the last. As we drove that long lonely road out of Hatfield cove, perched on my knees in the seat, peering back over the window through the trees and dust and watching the sunset, it wasn't just the day slipping away—my soul felt a little lost somehow.

I knew if the events of the day were to be talked about, it would be me to bring them up. It has always been that way. The rest of my family just doesn't up and talk about difficult things without provocation. The only thing I knew for sure was that if my parents had known the "grape juice" was the least bit intoxicating, they would have refused it. I'm confident it was the only time in their lives an alcoholic beverage touched their lips.

Later that evening, lying in bed and listening to the rat-tat-tat of rain hitting our tin roof, tired of my inner

13

struggle, I lapsed into a weird nothingness. It felt like someone had died.

Mom has always served as my confidante if I asked, so at goodnight time, I haltingly tried to describe my feelings. She said, "Don't worry, it's probably something called depression. It's perfectly natural and should go away soon. In fact, I'm feeling a little depressed myself." She brought her well-worn Bible to me, saying her remedy for depression was to read the Psalms. Little did either of us realize, that discomfiting feeling she called depression, was the first of several intense emotions that would haunt me throughout life.

The depression did go away—for a while—and a few weeks later, this lad got another taste of anointing. But this time it wasn't fermented juice; it was the real thing. You see, the only intoxication we were permitted was what Dad called the Holy Ghost.

This might be a good time to explain that my dad was not just any preacher—he was a *Pentecostal* preacher. And if that weren't enough, he was a Pentecostal preacher in the extreme sub-culture of the Appalachians. The world of holiness juxtaposed with the clannish mountain customs made for an explosive mix, as "outsider" preachers like my dad brought them old-time religion with an exciting new twist. Combined with the new-fangled invention called television, the contrasting worlds of Hollywood and religion were ruthlessly and relentlessly causing a ruckus among the mountain folk.

Their deep, almost spiritual alienation toward change cannot be overstated. They plied their meager existence toiling beneath the real world, protected from progress by endless hours in the darkness, rarely emerging from the mines or the dystopia of Appalachia. When a person rockets down a black hole into the abysmal unknown every day from before sun up to after sundown, the harsh light of change casts a horrifying glare. In fact, if Jesus Himself were to appear, bringing a bit of clay and spit, and offer to take away their blindness, they would likely say no.

I reckon that's why decades later, reading a vivid and haunting recounting of Vincent Van Gogh's heartbreaking attempts to minister to the people in the Borinage coal-mining region of Belgium, left me drained and numb for days. His early drawings capture the stark gray essence of a hopeless existence. I, like Vincent, realized later in life that even if the mountain people could do something else, they would not. Defying explanation, they loved their mines and most would rather be underground than above it. All they asked of life was a living wage, fair working hours, a home to live in, and a place to worship.

Sunday church services offered a safe and culturally acceptable reprieve from the monotony of everyday existence. And the new Pentecostal church services offered something that previously had only been found at the moonshine still. These services, complete with emotionally charged music and preaching, speaking in tongues, handling snakes, healing the sick, miracles, foot washings, and dancing in the Spirit, offered a much-needed escape from the cares and burdens of a dreary life. In much the same way spiritual songs offered American slaves freedom from the plantation fields, Pentecostalism offered ecstatic release from the somber confines of the mines.

This rowdy new way of worshipping God started just up the Appalachian mountain range in 1886. A holiness group fled the stale rituals of mainstream denominations calling themselves The Christian Union. A relative of mine named T.N. Elrod was one of seven charter members. Ten years later, the experience they called the baptism of the Holy Ghost lit their fire, as it were, and the rest is history.

Now called the Church of God, this small gathering of seven exploded over the next ninety years to a present-day membership of seven *million*. Blue-collar mountain communities provided fertile ground for a religion based primarily on emotional release, rather than rational theology. The passionate music evolved quickly into a hypnotizing mixture of hillbilly, black Gospel, and the older tradition of sacred harp and shaped notes.

15

You must experience a Pentecostal service deep in the Appalachian Mountains in order to believe it. And that brings me back to the "anointing."

One of the more memorable characters ever to attend one of the churches where my Dad pastored was Brother Jubal Whitener. He was large-bodied, ungainly, and socially awkward. There was not a tooth in his head and because of that, his speech was impaired. Standing over six-foot-four, he had a shaved head that always had a few prickly silver hairs sticking out in all directions, and he possessed the largest hands I'd ever seen. They always felt like dried-out leather. So it was unconscionable to me that he greeted the menfolk with the dreaded "wet fish" handshake. The wet fish comes with a limp wrist and a pathetic grip. Nothing is more guaranteed to ruin your reputation with me than a weak handshake. But I digress.

Dressed in his finest Liberty overalls, he would go 'round to the women folk, aiming to greet them with a holy kiss. You could see all the ladies scatter like chickens, filling their arms with a protective cover of screaming children, or suddenly feeling impressed to hurry to the altar for some preliminary praying. I suppose his holy kiss was to the women like his wet fish was to me. His reputation seemed tarnished, irrespective of gender.

About forty minutes into the service (you could almost set your clock to it), just as the singing was really getting emotional, Brother Whitener would spring a couple of feet in the air, deliver a war-whoop, and set off 'round and 'round the church, banging against the pews, upsetting the altar, and making general havoc. Next, he would run the tops of the pews full-speed, from the front of the church to the back, in a frenzy of ecstasy, with his hands up in the air and his voice speaking in tongues. To this day, I cannot explain why they didn't tip over.

He could not speak mountain jargon decently with his lack of teeth and all, and he couldn't read or write, so his best rendition of unknown tongues and heavenly languages was something like "tippee-toe, tippee-toe," over and over. Starting out slow and deliberate, it wouldn't take him long to get the "anointing." By that time, the tippee-toes were coming so fast, you could see sweat and spit flying all the way across the church.

He would then tear around the church again, spreading chaos and destruction in his path. I have actually seen him throw a few double somersaults, deliver a final mighty shout, and sail through an open window as gum-powered tippee-toes eerily reverberated throughout the church. My brother and I would sit there petrified with astonishment, warily peering over the shelter of our back pew, as various other people lay on the floor writhing in the Spirit and flush with anointing.

Somehow I never got to speaking in tongues but it wasn't for lack of trying. I remember as a very impressionable young boy, the church people praying over me at the altar until the wee hours of the morning, imploring God to give me the utterance.

Later, as a still impressionable but much older man visiting Italy, I implored the Lord to give me Italian tongues, so that I could properly order food and wine. I figured if the Lord could stimulate Brother Whitener to say, "tippee-toe," he could at least help me say, "ge-la-to" without the taint of a Southern accent.

17

# CHAPTER 3

# KITH AND KIN

My dad would often say he was raising us children under the admonition of the Lord. I wasn't quite sure what admonition meant, but it sure was tough being under it.

I have often contemplated how rational or even half-rational people could ever have lived under the heavy burden of admonition, considering its inconveniences; and how they had managed to carry such a cross when it was plain that what I had suffered for a while as a young'un, they had suffered all the days of their lives.

19

Don't get me wrong; ours was a loving family. But somehow, somewhere down the line, admonition came into the picture. I think it might have commenced with my grandmother Elrod. I don't know how *she* came to be under it; but trust me, her parents obviously saddled her up with a powerful load. Inherited religion is a curious thing, and interesting to observe and examine, because the prejudices of one's breeding are not gotten rid of very easily.

My memories of my grandmother are quite vivid. We called her Nanny. She had the sort of mouth that turns down; and even on the rare occasions when she would smile, the structure of her mouth made it look like a frown. Maybe that's why she never appeared happy. In fact, there was an anger about her that only comes when people carry too much advice.

I'm afraid this admonition was much harder on the womenfolk than us men. Now I'm not saying it was easy for anyone, but being an old-time Pentecostal woman came with a heavy burden.

Nanny was tall for a woman and right stocky. She always wore knee-length cotton dresses, gray rubbery work shoes, and shiny hosiery—even on days hot as hell. There were lots of long black hairs on her unshaven legs and they would protrude randomly through the nylon. Her pretty hair streaked with silver was always hidden away in some sort of bun and hairnet.

Her temper wasn't hidden though. I recall one day she came home early from work at the yarn mill with a big white gauzy bandage on her hand. When the story was finally sorted out, it seemed that some coalminer's daughter at the mill had dared try to cross her.

We questioned her as to the particulars and then listened as if the story had been a page out of the Gospel. She took to storytelling like a duck to water; there was a preacher concealed in her, sure. It was easy to see where my daddy's oratory skills came from.

She described the fight in much the same way he would deliver a sermon on Sunday. It was as if life went boiling through her veins, and she seemed like a new woman. In a voice deep, measured, and charged with doom, she began, and rose by dramatically graded stages to a colossal climax.

It seems a young hussy named Violetta had been agitatin' Nanny for quite some time. (We kids could've told Miss Violetta she was cruisin' for a bruisin'.) The disagreement started tamely enough with the usual bickering and jostling around the time clock, but for some unknown reason, it quickly escalated to a full-scale misunderstanding, replete with hair pulling in the break room and culminating with a catfight conducted with scissors. That Jezebel obviously didn't know her Bible history and therefore underestimated the raw power of repressed admonition. It was shades of Mr. Hatfield. When it was over, Nanny went back to work and Violetta didn't. When the wounds finally healed, she decided to find work elsewhere.

Not only did Nanny possess a penchant for scissors, but she also had a knack with hickory switches. There was nary hesitation in applying them liberally to her grandsons, most times without apparent cause or reason. As we screamed our innocence of whatever mysterious affront we had evidently caused God, she would say as she flayed our tender hides, "Well, if you'uns didn't do something this time, this here's for the time you did." Arguments have no chance against this logic.

The hickory switches came from a tall hedge that ran alongside the house, and as I grew older, she had the audacity to make me go and fetch my own switch, strip off the tiny green leaves, and hand it to her so she could— what she called—"strop my hide." Many times my brother Terry and I would rush to the screened-in front door with tears and gnashing of teeth as my parents returned, showing our red welts and begging them to never, ever bring us to Nanny's again. My brother and I did tend to fight a lot, so I reckon they figured we got what was coming to us.

It was along about that spanking era I determined to think out some way to reform this perditious evil called admonition and somehow influence the people of the

21

world to let this foolish way of thinking die out. But as much as I hated that house of inquisition, one thing always brought me back. It sat catty-cornered on the right just as you came in the front door. It was a magical wooden box that mysteriously captured light in a tube and transmitted it in a series of individual lines of beams. It would then magnetically deflect each line one at a time so that it formed a moving picture. This hypnotic contraption was called an electronic television.

Somehow Nanny had acquired the only one for miles. And no amount of "stropping" could keep me away. In fact, we kids would walk the extra distance in the heat after school just to have a few minutes situated in front of this magical invention. I would sit motionless, steeped in satisfaction, drunk with enjoyment. Yes, this was heaven. As I think back, the only tolerable memories I have at Nanny's place were late afternoons when the tiny fuzzy gray-and-white screen fluttered. It emitted an aura that caused even Mrs. Admonition herself to sit peaceably for hours in mesmerized silence, grasping for a few moments of guilty pleasure.

Religion caused lots of guilt around the mountains and pleasure was hard to come by, so about the time I was six years old, the continuing story of *Peyton Place* caused ripples in more than just the virgin air waves of Appalachia. This nighttime soap opera stretched the boundaries of what was considered morally acceptable in the pre-sexual revolution 1960s. Extramarital affairs, unwed teen pregnancies, family betrayals, mental illness, and even murder were all lurking behind the storybook façade of this picture-perfect, centuries-old village and its citizens. Why, it was like the Bible stories that were always hushed up in church had suddenly come to life.

After sneaking and watching a few episodes of *Peyton Place* through a crack in the bedroom door when we would stay the night at Nanny's, it dawned on me that I might not have to shoulder the full burden of reforming admonition by myself after all. It seems I had been miraculously granted an unlikely partner in the electronic television.

Then two years later, after Nanny solicited a solemn vow not to tell my dad, I was finally allowed to watch *Dark Shadows*. Each afternoon I would join the 175-year-old vampire named Barnabas Collins in search of fresh blood and his lost love, Josette. When the music began and waves thundered into the cliffs beneath Widow's Hill, for a few short moments, I would escape the confines of poverty, coal mines, and religious control into the magical realm of Colinsport; replete with witchcraft, spells, and vampire bats summoned from hell.

My grandpa (we called him Papa, pronounced pow-pah) obviously knew a thing or two about hell. He lived in the same house; although not in the same bedroom as Nanny. I have no earthly idea how they got hitched. They were a couple of people who came together with great random. My granny was chock full of admonition and was old before her time, while Papa was full of wildness and youth.

He was a short and brawny man with muscular arms developed by years of work as a stonemason. A balding pate crowned a weathered and leathery face, and he had thick lips that my dad's sister, Aunt Mary Jane (we kids called her Jane Jane) inherited. There was a round growth of skin on the right side of his nose that looked like a pea and his Herculean strength was exceeded only by his unpredictable temper. One could tell by the intense look in his eyes not to take him lightly, and by his gait that he was satisfied with himself.

George Washington Elrod, my grandad, will always be an enigma to me. If Mom pondered how she birthed me, then I'm sure she has given considerable thought to the sheer odds of how Papa begat my Dad. They were a study in contrasts.

My grandfather was a man full of passion. It seeped from his pores like lava from a volcano. I'm betting there was a fiery eruption when he met Nanny for the first time. He was twenty and she was all of thirteen when they married. Papa took her out of an intolerable situation.

My great-grandparents were moonshiners and always *piled up with trash* (see page 9: mountain jargon.) The

23

men who circled their home like vultures were not beneficial to a pretty young girl smelling of innocence and womanhood. The Appalachian Mountains were full of ancestral blood that was rotten with this sort of unconscious brutality, brought down by inheritance from a long procession of rednecks who had each done their share toward poisoning the stream.

When a child gets the magic stripped right out of their soul by evil too hard to understand, the admonition of the Lord with all its rules and regulations provides safe confines. But the stone walls of old-time religion are hard to escape, its mortar filled mostly with judgment and little grace.

There is a big difference between forgiveness and reconciliation, and somehow I don't think Nanny was able to reconcile the abuse of her childhood. Her heart had hardened toward both the good and the bad.

Papa's wildness and youth probably longed for her to break out of this unjust captivity, but to Nanny it was insult and outrage, and a thing not to be countenanced by any conscientious person who knew their duty to a sacred belief.

It is an old and weary tale. They fought and struggled and succeeded; meaning by success, that they lived and did not die. For Nanny, simply existing was enough, but for Papa it just wasn't.

He taught himself to read and write. I remember taking my ruled manuscript paper with the dotted line in the middle and holding his big rough hand in mine as he haltingly scrawled his name. We would write with the red scratched-up flat carpenter's pencil that he used to mark the rough surfaces of his stones. It was easier for him to grip than my little round school pencil. Before that time, Mom and Dad would help him write an "X" as his signature on legal documents.

My grandfather couldn't write very well, but he sure could tell a fine story. Nanny was not the only one who gave Dad his preaching genes—my father inherited a double dose of oratory. All one had to do was get Papa started and he would work around to his own history for a text and himself for a hero, and then it was good to sit there and hear him spin.

He would tell how he had begun life as an orphan without money in 1913, without family or friends able to help him; how his sister Fanny was displaced; and about another sister they never found. How his day's work was from sixteen to eighteen hours long, and yielded only enough food to keep him in a half-fed condition; how his faithful endeavors finally attracted the attention of a good stonemason, who came near knocking him dead with kindness by suddenly offering, when he was totally unprepared, to take him as his apprentice for three years and give him board and clothes and teach him the trade— or "mystery" as the freemasons called it. Self-made man, you know.

That was his first great rise, his first gorgeous stroke of fortune, and he couldn't speak of it without a sort of eloquent wonder and delight. Because of his work, he wasn't able to go to school, but he did make enough money to travel. He even went as far as the western seaboard.

Papa was the first and only Elrod besides me who learned how to swim. The admonition of the Lord frowned on "mixed bathing," but somehow when he was about sixteen, before he got hooked up with Nanny and her religious caution, he was a hobo and would jump trains to California. I don't know what he did—he would never say —but one thing he learned was how to swim like a fish in those waters they call Pacific.

At the age of ten, I remember taking our first-ever family vacation to the faraway state of Florida in our old Chevy station wagon. It may as well have been Europe. We kids were beside ourselves with excitement and Papa went with us.

Mom fixed sandwiches and we would stop at picnic tables along old Dixie Highway and U.S. Highway 41. The network of highways called the Dwight D. Eisenhower National System of Interstate and Defense Highways, and specifically Interstate 75, was still some ten years from completion.

There was also no such thing as air conditioning in a 1957 Chevrolet, but since we had never experienced it, we didn't even miss it. All the windows were down and the breeze flowed through the car and cooled our skin. It would cause serene waves of satisfaction to roll over my soul. Until we got to Florida, of course, and then it just made us hotter. But we didn't care; we just marveled at the sights and delights of traveling to a new and foreign land.

Mom brought cups for Terry and I to pee in. She had learned the hard way on our trips to the city from the mountains that young boys had to go way too much. We would crawl to the back, our sister Cheryl would look straight ahead, and we would do our business. When Dad would stop for gasoline, we would discreetly empty our cups.

Now most people go to Florida for a few relaxing days of sun and fun on the beach. But not the Elrods. I will never forget seeing the beach for the first time; I gasped in awe. It was a bright, reposeful summer seaside, as lovely as a dream, and as busy as a Friday.

Terry and I rolled up our blue jeans—we were not allowed to wear shorts—and ran for the ocean flinging sand everywhere. On my way, I spied females sporting sweet outfits as ever I'd seen, what there was of them. I found myself staring wide and timorously, the picture of astonished curiosity touched with concupiscence. I moved along as if in a dream.

It's hard to imagine what other people thought as they saw us. Mom and Cheryl wading in their full-length dresses, Dad in his long pants and shirt sleeves, and us boys in our rolled-up jeans, skin white as ghosts, screaming Southern euphemisms.

Suddenly Papa stripped off his shirt, his workman's tan emphasizing his broad and naked torso. I will never forget it as long as I live. He jumped headlong into a crashing wave and began to swim out to deeper water. Terry and I marveled at the scene and I made a vow then and there to

26

one day learn how to master this amazing ability. After Papa swam for a few minutes and helped us learn how to surf the waves, we left the beach and proceeded to immediately drive the eleven hours back home. We had been at the beach for a grand total of one hour. But Dad, Mom, and Cheryl had had enough. They were ready to get away from the hot sun, sticky sand, and indecently dressed people. It was obvious they felt uncomfortable and out of place in their layers of clothing and religion. Papa and us boys begrudgingly took our places back in the car.

A normal person might suppose our trip was cut short because we didn't have money to stay in a motel, and that is probably correct—but it's not just that. It's about the journey, not the destination. It's always been that way with my dad. He's often said he could have been a truck driver. For him, it was more important getting there than being there. I reckon there's some good in that thinking somewhere; but somehow it didn't seem right to just up and leave something that beautiful and soothing after only a few short minutes. Try as I might, I couldn't make heads nor tails of it.

Getting back to my grandfather—in today's medical vernacular, my Papa would probably be labeled bipolar. He was pulled one way by Jekyll, the other way by Hyde. The same man who would gently hold my hand and listen quietly as I read to him and helped him write, would embarrass the fire out of me when I accompanied him in public. He would start fights without provocation. It seemed that every trip with him to the flea market turned into a brawl. To the unconsciously indelicate, all things are delicate. Papa was not aware of his indelicacy and I had the presence of mind enough not to mention it.

There were many times Nanny would throw him out of the house because of his drinking binges, and I remember one time in particular when Dad had to go to a bar and physically drag him out. That night was my first time to experience a drunken person. Dad did not allow drinking in our home, so Papa would gradually sober up, and Nanny would let him come back to their house. That pattern of

27

getting drunk, getting thrown out, living with us, and eventually moving back continued the rest of Nanny's life.

One final and bittersweet story about my Papa Elrod. Having read the Hardy Boy mysteries, I thought it high time Terry and I started a detective agency of our own. We called it the Elrod Detective Agency and we were constantly sniffing out danger and exploring the wild.

One region of intrigue at that time that we reckoned needed reconnoitering was the room out back Papa had been adding onto their tiny four-room house. He'd been working on that room for years, and to us it seemed a mysterious place. An old black tarp was loosely stapled to the entrance and the unlit space had not been finished out. It smelled of must and the walls were vertical slats of bare two-by-fours standing in contrast to the intricate spider webs hanging from the rafters.

The appointed day came and we slipped out back to "play." We quietly removed a few staples, stepped into the dark, and commenced our detective work. Earlier it had been determined to make a list of clues to aid in our deductions—just like the Hardy Boys.

Terry wielded a flashlight and I had a ballpoint pen and a clipboard holding a yellow legal notepad, complete with our agency logo meticulously drawn at the top. As we explored the secret space, we noticed an old trunk covered by a wheelbarrow. The location of the wheelbarrow was duly noted and being worthy detectives (and curious young boys to boot), we carefully moved the wheelbarrow and opened the heavy lid.

Inside the trunk was hidden treasure, but not the kind we expected. Being of the innocent and naive sleuth variety, our former experiences had not yet prepared us for a discovery of this magnitude. There were breasts everywhere—very large breasts on very naked and very beautiful women. Magazines filled the trunk. I started taking notes.

It seemed the temperature suddenly rose to a hundred and fifty degrees in that sweaty back room, and we could feel the devil's breath on our necks as we exchanged paralyzed expressions and gasped "oohs" and "ahs."

Even though Papa had recently learned to read, it was easy to deduce that that particular ability wasn't required for these glossies. And after much conscious rumination over the years—considering our religious constrictions on sex, his bipolar symptoms, and lonely bedroom—the contents of that trunk just seemed to add up.

That evening at home, enthusiastically and innocently reporting our findings to our parents, we unexpectedly encountered yet another one of those moments when everything got real quiet. I was beginning to realize I possessed a knack for creating voids in the air, but for some reason, Dad wasn't whistling this time and Mom's face was bright red. They were surprised into an uncomfortable shock, and obviously had no idea what to think or do about this hidden treasure. As far as I know, it was never mentioned again.

The average life span of an American male born in 1913 was fifty years and three months, and an American woman born in 1920 was expected to live fifty-four years and six months. The last nail was finally driven in Nanny's lifelong coffin at the age of fifty-five years and two months, and Papa defied all odds and lived to be almost eighty-seven.

About eight years after Nanny died, when Papa was around seventy, he took up with a toothless snuff-dippin' backwoods lady named Myrtle Roach. By that time, Aunt Jane Jane had gotten married and moved out, and Papa had finally been able to settle in and claim the house he had been kicked out of so many times as his own. I think his last years after Nanny died were the most peaceful of his life; he made peace with God, quit drinking, learned how to play the guitar, and would even preach sometimes at my dad's church. He loved to fish and met Myrtle one day while buying worms she had dug up and was selling for bait. She soon moved in with him and became his common-law wife. They were happy there for several years, but Myrtle wanted to live close to her family, so Papa sold his homeplace and used the money to build her a house in

29

Roach Hollow. He constructed it with his own hands from the ground up in his mid-seventies.

They started a new business selling leather goods and throw rugs and just about any other trinket you could imagine. He and Myrtle would also sew pillows, selling them at the very same flea market where he used to beat people up. Every time I would visit them, Papa would try to sell me a throw rug or a leather belt.

Those occasional visits to Roach Hollow (at that time I lived near Jupiter Island, Florida, which has the second highest per capita income of any inhabited place in the country) created another one of those cataclysmic fights between my reason and my consciousness. My new life in the Palm Beach area with its excess and affluence just did not add up to the extreme poverty in which Papa and Myrtle lived.

It would almost suffocate me going into the squalor of his dark one-room house piled high with junk. It smelled of smoke, sweat, and God knows what else. To calm this internal malaise, I slowly but surely began to repress where I came from.

Papa would probably still be alive to this day, but he misbuilt the fireplace in his new home, and it constantly drafted into the house. When we would visit and try to tell him about our worries of carbon monoxide, he wouldn't (or couldn't) listen. The doctors listed cause of death as old age, but I think his dad-blamed stubbornness eventually got the best of him.

# CHAPTER 4

# MOM AND DAD

The knowledge and wisdom our parents and grandparents pass down matters, but what we learn from *who they are* matters most. Where Papa would have been storming the temple, turning over tables, and beating up the moneychangers, Dad would have been patiently putting up with the wanderings of the children of Israel for forty years and sending them manna. If God had become a man instead of Jesus, he probably would have been my dad.

Now if you think I'm saying my dad is perfect, think again. I'm not holding that cursed expectation over anybody, much less my father. He has his foibles just like you and me. But regardless of what he thinks—with that blasted Pentecostal belief that you can fall from grace— he's going to heaven, whether he believes it or not.

31

To give some perspective to this story, Papa learned to write with his right hand; my dad writes with his left. And then I came along writing with my right, and I suppose if I had had a son, he would be writing with his left.

Where Papa was hot-tempered and unpredictable, Dad was even-keeled and steady. Where Papa was easily distracted, Dad was focused. Papa had an inflated self-esteem; Dad was humble almost to a fault. Papa was loud and boisterous; Dad was quiet and soft-spoken.

Until, that is, he stepped up to what he called the "sacred desk." Straightaway his mercury went up to the top of the tube, and his solicitudes all vanished. The unassuming man we all knew and loved, when behind a pulpit, miraculously became a Holy Ghost–filled oracle of God. For a few short moments, he would be the center of all heaven's wonder and reverence.

My reason would hear a man quoting an entire book of the Bible as though it were a seven-digit phone number, but my consciousness would see a man shouting and speaking in unknown tongues. He poured out volumes of speech to match, and contorted his body and sawed the air with his hands in a most extraordinary way. At the end of sixty minutes, he would drop down panting and exhausted.

He would rail against sin as eloquently and fiercely as the most passionate hellfire and brimstone preacher, and yet I've witnessed that same man reason in calm and patient tones with a threatening coal miner crazed with moonshine. I've seen him preach so hard that his false teeth went flying across the church, and yet I've seen him gently mentor and encourage young preacher boys around the intimacy of our kitchen table. I've seen him work two and three jobs in order to better serve his parishioners, only to have those same people ride roughshod over him because he wouldn't live in the ramshackle and dilapidated house where they wanted him.

I witnessed with my own eyes a lunatic mountain lady attack and hit Dad with a family Bible while he was in the pulpit, trying to cast the demons out of him. She and her friend Delsea were furious because Dad had preached the

Sunday previous using the text of 1 Corinthians 14:40: "Let things be done decently and in order."

He was addressing the fact that every Sunday morning in that little forty-member church, the two of them would get up to sing (you must understand that in our Pentecostal tradition, anybody and everybody who felt God leading them to sing got to sing, whether God had anything to do with it or not) and the "Spirit" would take hold of them and they would wail, dance, and show off sometimes for an hour or more 'til nobody was left but us five Elrods and the two of them.

Dad finally got tired of their charades (not to mention he had to play piano for them the whole dad-burned time) and decided to publicly address the fact that church should be somewhat more orderly. That is when they decided to take the Bible and cast him out. Sometimes there is no accounting for human beings. There are times when one would like to hang the whole human race and finish the farce.

Those backwoods people eventually ostracized Dad to the point that we moved down to the big city for a while to take a rest. The Lord's work can be mighty trying at times. It seems that most churches I've known are filled with rejects from normal life and little people who finally have a chance to act big, even though they haven't earned the right to wield power in real life. A little power is a strange thing, and a little religious power can be downright mean. More than once I've seen a deacon who had gotten his brother at a disadvantage stop to pray before he cut his throat—figuratively speaking, of course.

I once heard an old black preacher, Dr. F. G. Sampson, tell this story: "General God went to Captain Jesus and asked him to send Lieutenant Holy Spirit to the barracks to make sure the Christian troops were ready for battle against the spirits of darkness. Lieutenant Holy Spirit came back and somewhat reluctantly said, 'Sir, I'm sorry to report that we are unfit for duty.' General God replied, 'Lieutenant, why is that? Are we worn out from warring against the Devil and his legions?' The Holy Spirit replied,

33

'No, sir. We're not ready because we are so bruised and battered from fighting among ourselves.'"

Dad believes in fighting for what's right, but when it came to family, he didn't cater to disagreements. One Sunday afternoon at Nanny and Papa's, we kids were watching the electronic television, paying no mind to the normal shouting and arguing that frequently happened between Nanny, Papa, and Aunt Jane Jane.

Evidently Nanny and Jane Jane had tried to spread their malignant admonition by ridiculing Mom's attempt to style her hair in the latest fashion. As tears silently coursed down Mom's cheek, Dad quietly pushed his plate forward, got up, took Mom in his arms, and walked out with us kids in tow. As that now-familiar quiet permeated the car, Dad drove away.

A few blocks down the road, he pulled over to the side of the road and laid his arms and head on the big steering wheel of his beloved Chevy and began to sob. Mom gently and tearfully placed her lovely arm around him and waited until he was through. Except for family funerals, it was the only time in my life I saw him cry. His grace and long-suffering would eventually get the best of him, and we would always return to Nanny's and it would be as if nothing happened. To Dad, family is family, no matter what.

The church people and now his own flesh and blood had sapped the strength right out of him. As he wearily raised his head, he turned to us and softly said, "We will *not* raise our voices in our home; we *will* treat each other with respect and love. I cannot control what goes on in that house, or the church, but I can say what goes on in our home." It was the most powerful sermon I ever heard him preach.

Dad's character and family values have always been an inspiration and example to me. But somewhere down the road of life, an unacknowledged yet mutual agreement developed between Dad and I not to talk about religion or church. Even though we love and respect each other dearly, as I became a man with my own ideas and perceptual view, our inherited stubbornness and growing disagreements in theology, life philosophy, and church methodology created a rift that caused friction when we were together.

Thankfully, we somehow realized the need to focus on the things we mutually understood and agreed on—the important things in life—like family, how the Braves are doing, and our shared love for music, gadgets, and electronics. Dad also loves to live vicariously through my travels. One of my greatest joys in life is regaling him with stories about places he will never see.

Dad attended my first-born daughter's wedding and was ready to leave five minutes into the reception. I tearfully begged Mom to have him stay, if only long enough to hear my words of tribute to my daughter. Heeding Mom's pleas, he stayed for my blessing, but left immediately after. His departure and inability to be present and savor one of the greatest moments in my life hurt desperately. Right or wrong, Dad is my personification of God, and I wanted him by my side to joyfully share this most sacred of times with me.

Talking to my first church "counselor" afterwards, he suggested it was because my success was too hurtful for Dad to face, so he did the only thing he knew to do—he just fled.

Seven years after that "wise counsel" and fifty-five years of life, I realize that wasn't it at all. My own hurt and disillusionment toward life after only thirty years of ministry must pale in comparison to Dad's, who spent over fifty years serving people with little if any acknowledgement. I suppose we have more in common than I realized.

He finally attended a Sunday service at my mega-church a time or two, and he didn't have much to say about it afterwards. There were more people in my orchestra than the entire attendance of his largest church. Try as he might, he simply could not grasp the thousands of people flooding the building each week. Like most things in my life, it was just too overwhelming for him to comprehend.

35

Almost from the beginning, the way we have experienced life has been so different. Psychologists say the most common problems between people are based on the assumption that we can guess what the other person is feeling and thinking. Dad and I just couldn't guess each other's thoughts, and we had no one to teach us the simplicity and power of honest debate.

It didn't help that I am part of the first generation in history (the generation of postmodern folks) who has the freedom both to know the rules and also to critique the rules at the same time. This self-awareness of a constant war between my consciousness and reason changed everything. I wanted to eat the fruit of the garden so I would know what it tastes like—and what I was missing if and when I decided to stop eating it. I loved the unknown, the unexpected, the allure of different cultures; and I began questioning authority and religious teachings at an early age. Dad loved the familiar, the habitual, his own group; and he was tied deeply to his early conditioning.

What little Dad understands about me comes about through the intercessions of my mom. If I can dare speak of Dad as God incarnate, then Mom is most certainly the Holy Spirit. From what I understand about theology, the Holy Spirit intercedes to God for groanings that cannot be uttered. Mom somehow innately understood much of the artistic angst in my being and she would gently help Dad put up with me.

My mother is a glorious amalgamation of her mom and dad—George and Katherine Daugherty. She's a jumbling together of extravagant incongruities, and a fantastic conjunction of opposites and irreconcilables.

Granny Katherine was of a light and laughing disposition; a bright, tiny, feisty, witty ball of fire whom everyone adored, especially her seven children. Nothing in this world was serious to her.

On the other hand, Pa Daugherty was of a scholarly but rigid temperament, tall and slender, dark and stoic, having spent much of his life serving as a combatant in the Navy during World War II and having those aforementioned children.

36

My brother, sis, and I didn't get to know Pa and Granny Daugherty like we did Papa and Nanny Elrod. Part of it was just sheer numbers. We were the only three grandchildren in the Elrod family, but we were among dozens in the Daugherty clan. They also lived a long way from the mountains in the east part of Chattanooga, and for a time in Arizona.

I remember having to be really quiet on our occasional visits to their modest but spit-shine clean house. Pa would be sitting tall in his easy chair usually reading, and did not tolerate much goings on. With his full head of coal-black hair, craggy nose, strong chin, and brown and gold skin—the color of a chestnut—he looked exactly akin to his rich American Indian heritage. Incidentally, both Pa and Granny are listed in the Native American census rolls. Pa worked as a Petty Officer in the Navy, then as a grocer, as a volunteer preacher, and at a lumberyard.

Much of what I remember about them comes from family stories. Mom has shown me letters Pa wrote to Granny from overseas during his service. They are eloquent, romantic, and poetic. His penmanship was excellent and his spelling flawless. It seems no coincidence that in high school, Mom won a national writing contest. They all loved to read and my mom loves to tell about holding a flashlight for hours under the sheets reading books because Pa's military discipline demanded a nine o'clock bedtime.

Somehow she went right from Pa's regulations to my Dad's legalism. It's sure tough to cut the strings to that damn admonition. But like Nanny, Mom was handy with scissors too. She just wielded them in emotional battles and psychological warfare instead of catfights. Many times Mom would plead my case to Dad. I'm sure Granny Katherine did the same pleading for Mom growing up.

My mom is soft, sensitive, and loving, with a sparkling spray of laughter. But she can also exhibit toughness, tenacity, and cunning. She sure has practiced a lifelong knack of knowing how to wrangle compromises for me from her rule-keeping husband and his inherited beliefs. Over and over, she would garner small victories in the battle for my freedom to escape the shackles of righteous admonition.

For some reason, a person's hair is irrevocably tied to religious fundamentalism. Nanny always kept hers in a bun or a hairnet, and Dad would constantly buzz mine off to a crewcut. My crying and screaming protests did not budge his intentions.

I'll never forget the smell and feel of that oily, metal shaver Dad would buy at S.S. Kresge. Much like Nanny did by making me go pick out the switch from the hedge, Dad would make me go with him to pick out a new shaver. He would straightjacket me in a plastic steel-gray cutting cape. Then paying no heed to my white-hot tears, he would cut until the heat of that instrument from hell matched the temperature of my grieving.

Much later in life, I learned that the shaving of one's head is a primitive method of subjugation. It is an act designed to be degrading and is a psychological tool to break down resistance and instill obedience. Young men (especially in the hippie era of the sixties and seventies) are very conscious and proud of their hair. It compliments one's face and adds to the good looks that are so important, yet so elusive, in those awkward adolescent times.

I don't really think Dad understood that by shaving my hair he was taking much of my manhood away, nor that he made me feel *ugly*. He was just doing what he had been taught by religion. My usually gentle Dad would seem to breathe fire and brimstone when he would say with a derisive sneer, "I'm not having a son of mine wearing those 'Beatle bangs.'" If words had been water, I would have drowned.

I've said before that religious ideas are curious things. They flow in ruts worn deep by time and habit, and the rare men (and women) who have the character to propose to divert them by reason and argument have a long contract on their hands. It's here you see the hand of that awful power, the fundamentalist church.

In the past hundred years, it has tried to convert a culture of innocent people into a culture of worms. Before the day of the Church's supremacy, mostly in the South, men were men, women were women, and they held their heads up and had pride and spirit and independence; and what greatness and position a person got, they got mainly by achievement, not by ordination.

But then the fundamentalist church came forward with an ax to grind; and she was wise, subtle, and knew more than one way to skin a cat—or a culture. She reinvented the "divine right of preachers," and propped it all around, precept upon precept, even with the Bible—wrenching from it it's good purpose to make it fortify an evil one. She preached (to the innocent) humility, obedience to superiors, and the beauty of self-sacrifice. She preached (to the innocent) meekness under insult; preached (still to the innocent, always to the innocent) patience, non-resistance under oppression; and she introduced disciplinarians and authoritarians, and taught all the Christian populations to bow down to them and call them Reverend.

But in a miracle comparable to Red Sea proportions, Mom gradually persuaded God, I mean Dad, to ease up on the hair. She realized his inherited admonition was spanking and churching the innocence right out of me, and if we were to maintain some sort of relationship as I grew older, the war of the haircuts would have to stop. This was just one of many intercessions she made that would change my life for the better.

Growing up as a very sensitive young boy, I was not allowed to play with dolls. They were supposed to be a girl's toy. Mom understood this not to be weird at all, but rather a temporary act of imagination that would develop my artistic and nurturing side. She interceded.

I was not allowed to watch television. Mom interceded.

I was not allowed to wear bell-bottom pants. Mom interceded.

I was not allowed to wear shirts with puffy sleeves. Mom interceded.

I was not allowed to wear shorts. Mom interceded.

I was not allowed to wear platform shoes. Mom interceded.

I was not allowed to go to the movies. I was not allowed to go to a pizza joint because they served beer. I was not allowed to go to "mixed bathing" areas. I was not allowed to dance (except, of course, in the Spirit at church). Sadly none of this changed while I was at home. Even Mom's intercessions could only go so far.

I was eighteen years of age before I saw my first movie, which, in an ironic twist of fate, happened to be Disney's *Song of the South*. I was eighteen before I had my first pizza, my first dance, my first swim, and my first taste of beer. Wine did not tickle my palate for another twenty years and I have yet to find the courage to put a cigarette to my lips. Those tentacles of religious rules have a way of reaching throughout time. Even today.

Religion, as I know it and as my parents know it, is a way of life where *no* is said with such constancy that on some days, one might forget that the affirmative is even a possibility. A fortunate few have been granted moms like mine, in part, to be relieved of all those endless *no's* of living a safe, responsible, productive, and moral life.

The question of restrictions, of what is allowed and not allowed, is very much at the heart of the story of fundamentalism. It is a parable about the nature of control. But what if the Garden of Eden was not a story of admonition at all? What if it was a story of getting it right by getting it wrong? What if it were truly a story of redemption? What if God is actually more like my mom than my dad? What if my dad was more like God before he got the innocence spanked and churched right out of him by religious admonition?

Mom tells the story of a boyfriend she dated previous to Dad taking her up in a small airplane, just the two of them. I can only imagine how the rushing air, the cramped cockpit, the adrenaline rush of the takeoff, and the happy sadness of the landing must have felt to a young, imaginative girl of fifteen. That was almost sixty years ago. Mom has never been in a plane since. Her allegiance and service to her husband, saddled with an inherited and unconscious religious fear, superseded the magic of her youth.

Ernest Hemingway wrote, "The best people possess a feeling for beauty, the courage to take risks, the discipline to tell the truth, the capacity for sacrifice. Ironically, their virtues make them vulnerable; they are often wounded, sometimes destroyed." Their entire being is reduced to a monotonous level of patience, resignation, and dumb, uncomplaining acceptance of whatever might befall them in this life. Their very imagination is dead. When you can say that of a person, he has struck bottom, I reckon.

I think religion has destroyed many people like that—people like my dad. Chains cease to be needed after the spirit has gone out of a prisoner. And somehow, innately, my mom fought to keep that from happening to me. She determined to save those microscopic atoms in me that were truly *me*.

Mom had a powerful capacity for sacrifice, but she never had that set expression of hopelessness, which is bred of long and hard trials and is an old acquaintance with despair. In fact, the only other time I saw her cry (besides church services and funerals, of course) was also in that ole' '57 Chevy. Most times, she bore up fine under all that life threw her way, but even Mom had her limits. Our first move away from family almost got the best of her.

We just thought times were tough in the mountains of Tennessee (and they were). We didn't understand just how good we had it until we moved to Arkansas in 1964. I was around six years old, Terry was five, Cheryl was three, and my parents were twenty-four.

Dad had gotten a wild hair and decided to move us almost five hundred miles away from home and was pastoring a tiny church in Batesville, Arkansas. When you compare the pay to the work required, you will quickly see that there's no money in church work. He was only making two or three dollars a week there, not nearly enough to feed a family of five, so he was futilely trying to find additional work elsewhere. That fateful three months we spent in the "land of opportunity" is the reason I can't eat black-eyed peas to this day. We existed on a diet of stale bread—we would have to scrape the mold off—and legumes for ninety days straight. We learned to dip our bread in the pea juice to soften it up.

We tried picking cotton. The endless fields of fluffy white looked like beautiful pink blankets as the sun would rise. That idyllic picture would quickly melt into wavy lines of heat as the blaze of an Arkansas summer day met the cooler air of morning. Each of us had a long narrow gunnysack that seemed to stretch forever. Cheryl was too young to pick, so she would sit on Mom's bag as it slowly dragged between the threadlike rows.

We would pick from sunup to sundown, our fingers raw and bleeding from the prickly bolls that protected the precious fiber. Mosquitoes would swarm to the sweat of our bodies each time we would remove a cotton ball. It was grueling work, especially for five- and six-year-old boys.

A completely filled-up sack would earn the sum total of 35 cents. We boys thought that was big money. And we loved the end of the day, because after weighing our bags and emptying them into a rickety cotton trailer on wheels, Terry and I would shimmy up the walls of chicken wire, balance on the narrow and shaky top, and take turns diving onto the pillowy laps of cotton. We would go headfirst, fall backwards with our arms wide, turn flips, and pretend we were flying in the clouds. On the quiet ride back to the parsonage, we would scratch our mosquito bites until they bled, and then fall in bed, only to start over again the next morning. We did this an entire summer until Labor Day.

With us boys back at school and just the two of them working the fields, seventy cents a day didn't cut it, even in the mid-sixties. Mom grew desperate and finally found a job at a chicken factory. She was issued a hairnet, a long white apron, and yep, a pair of scissors. I will never forget that instrument of death. They were big, thick, and very sharp—made of gray steel—and had a round ball on the end of one tip. Her job was to slice open wide the rear end of the chicken as it came down the conveyor belt. She would then use that metal ball to remove its innards, blood and guts spurting everywhere. When we would pick her up after eight hours of that grisly work, her hair and face would be covered in blood.

42

One fateful day, as she wearily got into the car, exhausted and smelling like pus and dead chicken tissue, the bloody track of a tear was evident on her face. (The sign of a tear on Mom's face was as demonstrative as the most boisterous shout Dad could muster on Sundays.) It was yet another one of those dead quiet times in the car. After what seemed an eternity, she gathered herself and softly said, "George, honey, I don't think I can do this any longer." It still wrings my heart when I think of it.

A kind man who had a grocery store across the street from our parsonage, who didn't even attend our church, gave Dad a few dollars for gasoline, and we quit Arkansas and headed back to the verdant hills and vegetable gardens of Tennessee that very next day.

Mom has given up a lot over the years to love and support my dad: her high school diploma, her writing, her airplane rides, her teenage years, and if truth be known, many of her dreams. But I believe she feels like she has gained far more than she sacrificed.

There have been many times during my travels later in life—gaping at the roaring and majestic Murchison Falls in Uganda, reveling in the historic and colorful Ponte Vecchio in Florence, savoring a romantic moonlit gondola ride in Venice, climbing a thousand-year-old tower in Kyrgyzstan, and snorkeling the indescribable Great Barrier Reef in Australia—I would think of Mom and wish desperately that she could experience these sensory delights alongside me.

If not for her encouragement and intercessions—finally kicking me out of the nest of illiteracy and privation—I would not have the ability to write these words. I would not have had the perceptual view necessary to experience a renaissance. And the rest of this book would just be a dream.

43

# CHAPTER 5

# IN PRAISE OF LATE BLOOMERS

I reckon I'm just getting started, not only with this book, but with life. You see, I'm what some people call a late bloomer. And nowhere is my late blooming capacity more evident than in my schooling.

When I was growing up in the Appalachians, I was always the smartest kid around. It was expected that I would do great things by my mom and dad, by my teachers, and most importantly, by me. I don't know whether that's a good thing or bad thing, but high expectations were always around me and for the first fourteen years or so, the results would seem to indicate that early success was a likely thing.

45

But after lots of good grades and academic achievement, the scholastic drive sort of died out. I hated high school and once in college, I found out that performing well wasn't always based on being smart. Study and regular, consistent academic effort was also required, and I'd never been asked to do those things.

I also had a lot of trouble in college with too many things to do—many of which didn't involve school or study. My dad felt it would be a good idea to do "real work," in case the schooling didn't pan out. So after a full day in class, I would pull a graveyard (third) shift at a yarn mill, and after a year or so of that, I eventually went to work at my first church. I also got really good at dating, playing softball, and making new friends. Before I knew it, I was on academic probation. Soon after that, I up and quit, and didn't get back to college until five years later, finally managing to graduate at age thirty.

Now there's at least a couple of reasons for my slow progress. One was the ongoing and frequent battles between my reason and my consciousness. This raging internal war slowed the normal pace of mental and emotional growth to a snail's pace.

I fought through those times, but just when I thought I was getting up to speed, my reason and consciousness would start screaming at each other about all the things I felt I was supposed to be, and the reality that I wasn't quite getting to the goals that had been expected. I wasn't becoming a doctor or an architect or a great scholar. I didn't end up teaching. I didn't go to the mission field. I didn't get a PhD or even a Masters degree. By my mid-twenties I was married with one child and had headed south to Florida in search of myself, barely managed to graduate with a Bachelor's degree in Music, and wasn't really sure where I was going next.

Another reason for my slow progression was because there was a dearth of true mentors and well-trained teachers in my life. Most of my guides were just dad-blamed useless.

Fortunately, there were five teachers who felt called to help shorten my learning curve. If not for them, forty years later, I would probably still be a redneck, living in the mountains, having never expanded my perceptual view. In other words, if not for them, I would have never known what I was missing.

The educators who influenced my life could not be more different: a rotund, balding old maid named Miss Sorrells; a tall, dignified black man with an afro named Mr. Thomas; a lecherous, chain-smoking band director named Mr. Batson; a soft-spoken missionary-turned-university–department head named Dr. Simoneaux; and a Juilliard School–trained vocal coach named Mr. Brown. These are the people who proved to be invaluable guides on my slow but sure journey to a renaissance.

One of my first memories of elementary school was being placed in a "gifted" class. This was about the time the American education system was trying to figure out how to provide an education to students who are now called "special needs" children. So they called them gifted. But, in the mountains in the sixties, we called those kinds of kids retarded—or worse. There was no filtering system, nor compassion among the roughneck kids I grew up with.

Now if you can picture a fair slip of a boy walking into class on the first day of school, wearing a big silly smile sort of like Gomer Pyle, talking incomprehensible jargon with an accent as thick as the mountains, and nary a measure of social skills, you might rightly understand why he could possibly be singled out for reassignment. First thing in the morning, on the second day of school, the teacher asked me to step outside, saying, "Honey, I'm so happy to tell you, you are being moved to what we call a class for the gifted. I'm sure you are going to love it."

Straight off, I was escorted to another room downstairs. As I walked the sterile hallway, I ruminated on how much I liked being described as gifted. No one had ever called me that before.

First thing I noticed as I entered the class was there were only half as many students, and three times the number of teachers. A very nice lady greeted me and

47

showed me to my desk. She had a dear face, talked really slow and distinct, looked me directly in the eyes, and possessed a nice smell and manner about her. She told me I was free to wander about the class, find a book that looked good, and locate a comfortable place to read. She said to take all the time I needed. There were shiny new books everywhere and I commenced to read them. It seemed like heaven.

About a week later, that nice lady came up, gently took my chin, looked me in the eyes, and said, "Randy, dear, just how many of these books have you finished?" I did my best to keep my eyes and voice from quivering, and answered, "All of them, ma'am." She abruptly dropped my chin. Things happened pretty quickly after that. It seemed that "all of those" books were supposed to have been enough to last each member of the class the whole year. Something wasn't quite right. I reckoned I wasn't gifted after all.

Next day, I was returned to my original class, the one for "normal" people, and to the same line of uncomfortable desks, sitting alphabetically and stuck somewhere between "D" and "F." There was only one teacher way up front who sat behind her desk and talked in a disinterested manner most of the day, without eye contact, to the thirty or so of us rowdy and smelly six-year-olds crammed in the room. Longing for the freedom of the "gifted" class, I was reminded not to move or talk, and the monotony dripped on for the next five years.

Not only was the magic in this boy's life being churched, barbered, and bullied out, I'll be if it didn't start getting schooled out too. That is, until we moved down to the city for a while, and I got promoted to junior high and the seventh grade.

As far as I can remember, it all started when our family moved to East Lake. This quaint inner-city neighborhood was a little over two square miles in area and as different from the wide-open mountains as daylight and dark. The population density was three times that of greater Chattanooga and was evenly distributed racially between black and white. Public education was administered by the

Chattanooga City School system and consistently rated the highest in all of Tennessee.

Being the oldest, it was my responsibility to walk with my brother and sister and make sure they were safely deposited at East Lake Elementary. As I separated from them, I could feel the sting of a tear moisten my eye. It was the first time going to a different school than my siblings. Ah, the pains of growing up.

Those days were the best and worst of times. Smack dab in youthful fantasies of Superman, Wonder Woman, and Bruce Wayne, I was also experiencing acne, body hair, and wet dreams. It was the agony and the ecstasy, the highs and the lows—the happy sadness of boyhood adolescence.

Outfitted with a dented purple Batman lunchbox containing a Spam sandwich and a Moon Pie, a stringy cloth three-ring binder, a new #2 pencil, straight-legged blue jeans with the cuffs rolled up, a tucked in blue-and-white plaid shirt, no-name tennis shoes, and crowned with a buzz-cut, I walked into the crazy confusing hallways of junior high.

It was 1971. Flesh and hair were on display everywhere. There was a certain manliness in the faces of the eighth-grade boys and most wore skin-tight bell-bottom pants, psychedelic tie-dyed t-shirts or dress shirts with puffy sleeves and ridiculously high platform shoes. The girls were a massed flowerbed of feminine show and finery. They were obviously immersed in a competition to see whose mini-skirt was the shortest and whose hair was the longest. As I stood there gaping in surprise and astonishment, I could feel my mercury rising.

As this new kid in town timidly walked into class, every eye seemed fastened upon me with severe inquiry and extravagant derision. But I was equal to the occasion. I determined to confidently locate my assigned seat between the D's and F's, and strike up a conversation with the person behind me. I sat down, turned around, and immediately felt as if I had been struck dumb.

Suzie Ezell sat behind me in the alphabet, and on that first day of seventh grade, she became the fairest thing on earth to me—roses, pearls, and dew-made flesh—a wonder-work, a masterpiece of God with eyes like no other eyes, a voice like no other voice, and legs like no other legs. To this day, when I catch a whiff of the Avon fragrance *Sweet Honesty*, my mind instantly flashes back to that singular moment of awe.

She had a freshness, a lithe young grace, and beauty that belonged properly to the creatures of dreams—and to no other. She set my heart to thumping. I found out that day you can't reason with your heart; it has its own laws and thumps about things which reason scorns.

I also found out a seventh-grade boy can't reason with his body. As Suzie smiled at me sweetly, blue eyes twinkling in amusement, she crossed her legs and her pink mini-skirt hiked up past the tops of her silk stockings. Suddenly it wasn't just my heart thumping. For the first time in my life, I was speechless. Hot blood was thumping in my temples, spreading a red flush across my face. Then it began forcing its way down to my nether regions. I hastily and strategically relocated my notebook. A husky voice intruded my reverie, "Mr. Elrod, would you kindly right yourself and see if you can manage to join us?"

As I "righted" myself, I quickly made up my mind to do two things: If the owner of that firm guttural voice was my teacher, I would straightaway learn how to please her. On the other hand, if the fantasy behind me was real, I would woo her passionately until she could do no less than succumb to my charms.

In due course, the teacher stood up in front of her desk with closed textbook in hand, forefinger inserted between its leaves, and commanded attention. When a good teacher makes their introductory speech, a textbook is as necessary as is the inevitable Bible in the hand of a minister who stands on the platform and preaches at church—though why is a mystery; for neither the textbook nor the Bible is ever referred to by the orator.

This particular teacher was a rotund creature of indeterminable age, with short thinning hair styled in oily waves; she wore a soft pastel cotton shift that accented her abundant girth. It hung like a shapeless gunnysack and covered her from neck to ankle. Her double chin was indistinguishable from her neck, and she had short stubby fingers. Elizabeth Sorrells held teaching in such reverence, and so separated it from worldly matters, that unconsciously to herself, her classroom voice had acquired a peculiar intonation that was like a preacher praying on Sunday. She began in this fashion:

> Now students, in this class you will sit up as straight and as tall as you can and give me all your attention. There—that is it. That is the way good boys and girls should do. I see one boy looking out of the window at the park—I'm afraid he thinks I am out there somewhere—perhaps up in one of the trees making a speech to the little birds. (The room filled with apprehensive twitter.) I want to tell you how good it makes me feel to see so many bright, clean faces assembled in class, learning to do right and be smart.

It was a pattern that would not vary and it became very familiar to us all. The latter part of the speech was marred the very first day by an event the likes of which I had never witnessed. She stopped in mid-sentence, waddled down the row of desks, and up to the biggest boy in the class—I later found out his name was the same as mine, and I was ashamed he bore it—the bully. Everyone was afraid of him. Everyone, that is, except Miss Sorrells.

She reached that short stubby hand down in the depths of her shift and slowly and dramatically pulled out a red rubber band. Before anyone could gasp, she held it high for all to see and then took a handful of his hair, his "Beatle bangs," banded them together, and arranged them to the side of his face. As she completed her task, she told us it was not permissible to block the clear vision of one's eyes with hair in her class. Beaming a commanding presence worthy of a general, she warmed herself in the sun of her own power and began to thunder and set forth the remaining rules of her domain.

51

It is not necessary to set down the rest of the oration. Suffice it to say, she dictated those first three periods called "morning block" like the despot she was. But we students discovered underneath all that blather and bluster was a huge heart and a passion to instill knowledge. The boy whose history this book relates blossomed under her tutelage. Two stories in particular come to mind.

Upon entering seventh grade, I had already developed an artistic penchant for adding curlicues to my longhand writing. But that would not pass muster with Drill Sergeant Sorrells. Many of my early papers would be handed back with a 100 firmly marked through with a red pen and replaced with a lower grade. Even though every answer was correct, she would ruthlessly take off four precious points for every violation of the standard cursive method of writing. I can still hear her preach, "As you write stories and essays for school papers and tests, it is important that your handwriting flows easily."

She should be proud of herself, now in whatever upper level of heaven great teachers find themselves. To this day, when people see my handwriting they compliment my penmanship.

As that fateful school year was drawing to a close, at a time when a young boy's forehead burns with the fever of spring, we were told there would be a special assembly for the giving out of awards. Walking in as usual, the first thing I noticed was my mom sitting in the back row. I just knew I was in some kind of trouble.

Without my knowledge, Miss Sorrells had urged her to take off work to be at the assembly. It was one of those fateful days that happen rarely in a lifetime. As the awards were given out, my name was called again and again: the current events award, Daughters of American Revolution history award, the Bible award (yep, believe it or not, public schools once taught the Bible), the citizenship award, and several others. Neither I nor my mom had any idea about the awards; Miss Sorrells had simply told my mom it was important that she attend.

To this day, I'm thankful for a caring teacher who took initiative to have Mom's attendance make a rare and special day even more meaningful. Throughout my lifetime, my parents were unable to attend most of my performances and ceremonies. Their work schedules made it seemingly impossible. They felt that providing a living for the family was more important than their presence at school and extracurricular events. But a portly, blustery, seemingly hard-hearted seventh-grade teacher made the awards ceremony (and that awkward adolescent year) magical.

My eighth-grade history teacher was a study in contrasts to Miss Sorrells. He was tall, handsome, distinguished, articulate, and always dressed in the latest fashion. But perhaps more importantly to my perceptual view, he was black.

Before our relocation to the city, I had never seen a person of color. I had only heard about "them." And let's just say what I heard was not flattering. The rampant racism and widespread ignorance in the Appalachian Mountains would not tolerate diversity. Where I was raised, a black person would have been shot on sight, black dogs were named *Nigger,* and the stores and public water fountains had "whites only" signs. I remember once asking my dad why a new store had been burned down in one of our rural mountain towns, and was summarily told that a colored family had tried to move in.

To my surprise, at the outset, Mr. Thomas captured my mind—and my heart. I can still see the shining beads of hair oil on his large and perfectly coiffed afro, his wide burnt sienna shirt lapels overlapping his dark brown sport coat, his brown-and-white-checked bell-bottom slacks and three-inch multi-colored platform shoes, and smell his musky cologne as he would walk between the rows of desks while enthusiastically gesturing and hypnotizing us with stories way too interesting to be labeled history.

He was the first teacher to make learning fun. We were assigned to quiz teams of five students each that would compete all year, culminating with a team champion being crowned at the end of the year. He announced he would personally take the winning team members on a field trip and would treat each one to a malted milk shake, French fries, and a hamburger.

Miss Sorrells had already taught me that I thrived in a well-disciplined classroom, but Mr. Thomas took learning to a whole new level. Where she fanned the flames of my thirst for knowledge, he created a veritable forest fire.

My team won the championship and Mr. Thomas was true to his word. It was the best burger, fries, and shake I've ever had. As he relaxed his academic posture and professionalism at the drive-in restaurant and chatted about everyday things, my consciousness realized he was not only the most intelligent and charming man I had ever known, he was also a person just like me—regardless of the color of his skin.

A battle of stratospheric proportions once again raged between my reason, which had been told people of color were inferior and incapable of intelligence—unworthy to associate with white folk; but my budding consciousness realized Mr. Thomas represented the ultimate rebuttal for the racist and ignorant line of reasoning I had been raised to believe. The world seemed to shake on its very foundation as I began to realize for the first time that my parents and church were fallible and subject to mistake.

This racially charged atmosphere, combined with a conscious knowledge that something was desperately wrong with unreasonable prejudice of any kind, propelled me into my first experience as a leader. As a fourteen-year-old social misfit, I empathically (and unexpectedly) found the inner courage to run for student council to lead a fund-raising campaign for our beloved black janitor "Muscles" Heath to pay his medical bills while fighting cancer. This "unusual" concern for a black man by a white student landed me on the front page of the very newspaper I delivered as a much younger boy.

It also led to an appointment to a joint steering committee composed of students and faculty members of Chattanooga City Schools charged with working toward better racial and academic understanding. A life pattern was emerging—even though I had no idea at the time; my

54

empathy and growing consciousness when confronted with need translated to passion, action, and leadership.

This convergence of strong empathic gifts and growing victories of my consciousness over reason were creating a leader and mentor in the making, but as with any great strength, it also comes with great weakness.

One perfect spring morning before school as the sweet smell of honeysuckle filled the air, the concrete playground was teeming with kids playing tetherball, jump rope, and my favorite game, "two-square." The game consisted of hitting an inflated red semi-soft rubber ball with small dimples back and forth in a rectangle divided into two equal parts. It scored much like table tennis. Competitors would wait in line, the game would go to eleven, and the winner would then take on the next person.

That fateful morning, Leroy Sample was the reigning champ and I was next in line. Leroy was big, loud, and a fierce bully. He was playing another boy and suddenly screamed at him for cheating. A moment later, he pounced on the smaller kid and began to pummel his head mercilessly.

As I watched Leroy hit the boy's head over and over with all his might, I suddenly became sick. It was as if Leroy was hitting me. I could viscerally feel the punches and the pain as the skull helplessly smashed into the concrete with each blow. Teachers quickly broke up the fight, and the kid was rushed to a hospital. I plodded through that day at school in a daze. I simply could not function. The dead look in Leroy's eyes as he beat the younger boy's brains out with his fists haunted me for days.

My all-too-frequent companion—depression—wrapped me up in its debilitating clutches, and rendered me helpless. I had no one to talk to, and as my reason and consciousness fought to sort this injustice out, I slowly began to retreat within myself. I could not risk the embarrassment of company.

I wanted to punish people like Leroy, to put reason before consciousness, justice before love; my mind would approve, but my heart would reproach me. If I possessed the myriad days this lifelong struggle has stolen from me, I would be years older and wiser. In this case, someone else punished Leroy. He was found beaten to death at the age of fifteen.

A few days later, I learned we were moving yet again. Forced busing (desegregation) zoned our neighborhood for either Kirkman Technical High School or Howard High School. Both were plagued with racial unrest as Chattanooga continued to experience race riots. My parents felt it best for our safety to move back to the protection and insulation of the backwoods as I entered high school.

I left East Lake Junior High having accomplished one of the two goals I had set upon entering that very first day. I had won Miss Sorrells over and it's safe to say I did please her with my effort. But alas, although the fantasy sitting behind me was indeed a reality, the goddess Suzie Ezell never succumbed to my charms. She became a cheerleader, sharing lockers with the football quarterback. My meager existence was never acknowledged.

# CHAPTER 6

# IN PRAISE OF BLOOMERS

The move back to the country was not a good one for me. The county schools were years behind the city school systems. For the first time in my life, I was at the same school for four years straight, and one would think that would provide much-needed academic stability, but I cannot remember learning one thing in high school that contributed to my future studies.

The motivation to excel in junior high quickly became apathy and disgust at teachers who were poorly trained, if at all. To make things interesting, I took bets from fellow students at the beginning of the school year that I could sleep every day in class and still make an A in the course.

The sad truth is that I won every bet and not one teacher ever woke me from my lethargy.

Two things salvaged my high school years: my dad's old trombone—and believe it or not—a haircut. But more about the haircut later.

Dad wouldn't allow Terry and I to play football. He was afraid we would get hurt, so the only alternative for any sort of extracurricular activity was band.

The band director's name was Doug Batson. He was a short man with a slender frame, frizzy golden-brown hair, and a beard with a little goatee that protruded forward, much like his pot belly. He would wear striped bell-bottom slacks with a distinct pleat and some sort of booty shoes that curled up on the ends like an elf. In fact, if he had not been such a hairy creature and a chain smoker, he could have passed for a leprechaun.

Mr. Batson was earthy and I couldn't get enough of his uninhibited self. So in tenth grade, I immediately applied to be his fourth-period "band aid." I had never met a man like him. His voice was raspy from all the cigarettes and his breathing labored, but that did not stop him from rattling off the most colorful language I had ever heard. He was the first person I ever heard drop the "f" bomb. We nerds would gather in his office at every opportunity and he would regale us with stories of wine, women, and song.

To my utter shock, one day as a few of us boys who were ulcerating to be men gathered around his office, he leaned back in his office chair and propped his pointy boots on his desk, eyes closed and arms lazily crossed behind his head. He then proceeded to fantasize aloud in vivid detail about how groovy and luscious it would be if the curvaceous blonde twin sisters who were our band majorettes would one day shed their clothes and grace the pages of *Playboy*. You could literally feel the heat increase in that cluttered office.

Later that hot spring day, during my customary nap on a school desk, consciousness wrestling with reason, I wondered if being pure really meant being happy. I remember reading somewhere that "being good is a fearful occupation; men strain at it and sometimes break in two."[1] As my face lay against that sticky laminate desk top, fever prickled my cheeks, perspiration trickled down my legs, and I conjured beautiful (but sinful, oh how sinful) images of the twins who sat only a few seats away.

Young boys *do* love sin. Never doubt it, oh how they love it, in all shapes, sizes, colors, and smells. So when a boy's religion labels everything fun and beautiful as sin, it makes for big trouble come blossoming time. Sooner or later, natural God-given desire and passion are gonna sprout and bloom. And after considerable wrestling, I think it's far better to germinate those wildflowers at a young age rather than later in life when things are grown-up and complicated.

Doug Batson not only gave me food for my fantasies, but more importantly, he gave me visions for a future. The only thing he loved more than sin was music. And his passion for tunes was contagious. He scheduled field trips and I eagerly signed up for every one. I was working on weekends and finally had some money of my own, so I secretly ponied up for what were to be life-changing experiences.

He took us to see jazz greats Woody Herman and the Thundering Herd, Maynard Ferguson, and Bill Watrous, as well as new rock bands such as Blood, Sweat and Tears, Chicago, and the Doobie Brothers. I was mesmerized. These people made money—real money—being musicians and doing what they loved.

I couldn't understand how the church and my dad could call this captivating music "sinful." Heck, now that I think about it, everything Mr. Batson taught me was condemned as evil. Mine was not to reason why; I just knew my consciousness loved every satanic beat. I was sick and tired of being good and unhappy so I made up my mind that year to become a professional musician.

Around that same time, as fate would have it, I met Brad Outz. He was a charismatic eleventh grader who lived next door in our latest neighborhood. Even though I went

---

[1] Ray Bradbury, *Something Wicked This Way Comes.*

59

to the same high school for four years, we still moved three times. When we first moved back to the country from Chattanooga, all five of us lived in a tiny mobile home. Mom hated it, so we then temporarily moved to a rental property until Dad managed to save enough to buy a home.

Brad was a tall, slender, good-looking guy with straight natural blonde hair that hung to his shoulders and would swing as he walked. He always sported a ready smile and won my brother Terry and I as friends almost immediately.

To say he was different than any boy I had met while growing up in the mountains was an understatement. He played guitar (a beautiful yellow Fender Classic Telecaster), he drove a hip VW Beetle, religiously practiced Kung Fu, and was already honing his skills in what was to become his lifelong career as a hairstylist. Brad did not *cut* hair—he styled hair.

On a fateful autumn day in eleventh grade, with a few strokes of his scissors (for once, the scissors were a good thing), Brad changed my life forever. I had been transformed, as if by magic. Turning sixteen and owning a car gave me a taste of freedom and independence so, despite Dad's protests, I had already tried to grow my hair out. But one side was much longer than the other and just stuck out in a random manner. My unruly curls and cowlick didn't help matters; combined with a stubborn case of acne, I felt and looked like an awkward, ugly loser.

Brad wet my hair, held a few strands up between his fingers, and clipped them all the same length with his scissors as we listened to Gladys Knight and the Pips sing *Best Thing That Ever Happened to Me*. To his credit and my immense relief, he never picked up those damn clippers except to make sure my sideburns were even. Brad instructed me to wash my hair again, shake it, and let it dry naturally. He admonished me to never touch a comb again. The entire process took about fifteen minutes.

The next day at school, angels sang. A twelfth-grade goddess named Susan, who one day previous had not been aware of my earthly existence, asked if I could give her a ride home. As she slid in the car, all legs and flesh, a smell of summer, sweet as clover, honey-grass, and wild mint filled the car. The white cloth of her tiny lacy bloomers peeked from beneath her miniskirt as she crossed her legs.

I felt waves of dizziness as I grasped for my keys, and when I tried to say something, my tongue felt thick and useless. She was the first female other than my sister to grace the confines of my purple 1962 Pontiac Tempest Station Wagon. She would not be the last.

I quickly raced to make up for lost time. This late bloomer had not realized the sensual vacuum deep within —the voluptuous hollow, the prolonged emptiness which undulated from tip to toe—had been waiting to be filled with summer flesh. Studies were forgotten and all that mattered was quality time with the opposite sex that at long last recognized my existence.

The soothing music of Gladys Knight was soon replaced by the angst of David Bowie. My nerdy purple Pontiac station wagon was replaced by a sexy dark-green Buick 454 four barrel. Pretty girls, loud music, and fast cars created a rush of youthful passion that sated my lack of academic fulfillment.

Somehow Mom managed to slow me down enough my senior year to take off work one Saturday morning and take a college entrance examination she had heard about called the American College Test. Mom was so determined I take the exam, she personally made sure I was up in time, treated me to a good breakfast, drove me to the test location, and quizzed me about it on the way back home. I sped away and did not give it another thought.

Several weeks later, I was unexpectedly called to the school office and introduced to the guidance counselor—a position until that day I did not know existed. She informed me that my score on the ACT was the highest recorded in school history and that I could have expected to receive numerous scholarship opportunities, were it not for a mediocre GPA. After my freshman year and winning all the bets by making A's, I quit trying at all for good grades. I finished high school with a B average.

Without a word of advice, she gave me two unopened letters with my name addressed in care of the school. Inside the envelopes were two scholarship awards. One was from a college affiliated with our religious

61

denomination and one from a school way up north in Maryland called St. John's.

Reading the words in disbelief, the letters shaking in my hand and tears filling my eyes, the small private Christian college offered me a $4,800 full-tuition scholarship for four years and the St. John's letter offered a partial tuition award that was over $20,000. Tuition costs (excluding room and board) today for four years at St. John's exceeds $120,000. These bequests were totally unexpected and receiving that much money for just one simple test was impossible for me to comprehend.

A few weeks later in May of 1976, I walked across stage and became the first Elrod in our family history to graduate from high school. To this day, no other male Elrod has earned a high school diploma—much less attended a liberal arts college.

In those days, there was no Internet to research colleges and our guidance counselor was uncaring and untrained. It was not until over thirty years later, reading the introduction to Charles Van Doren's *The Joy of Reading*, that I realized the classical education of St. John's in Annapolis, Maryland, would have been the perfect fit for my voracious love of books, the classics, and art. But there was no one in my life to serve as a guide and the bloom of a renaissance was delayed yet again.

It was expected by my family that I go to our "Christian" college. It was a full scholarship, it was close to home, and most importantly, it was "safe." No telling what those Yankee heathens would try to cram in my head. Besides, St. John's sounded Catholic and everyone knew those liberals were a cult. If I went there, I'd probably come home with the mark of the beast—or worse.

By that time, I had already met the thirteen-year-old girl I was to provide for and marry when she graduated high school. So I did the expected thing and enrolled at the local college for the fall semester.

# CHAPTER 7

# COLLEGE DAZE

Imagine a thousand repressed teenagers raised by old-time Pentecostal parents whose only answer to everything has been a resounding *no*. Throw in a throbbing and evocative charismatic worship service three times a week at the required chapel. Add to the mix a little freedom, and you get an explosive climax.

It was a seething cauldron of young adults at the height of their sexual prowess. What went on at that little Christian college behind closed dormitory doors would have made Hugh Hefner blush. Never mind the details—it will save me the trouble to let you imagine them.

The standing joke around the college was that most of the girls were looking for an MRS degree and would go to any length to get it. The only problem was that females outnumbered men almost three to one. To make matters worse for the heterosexual ladies, almost every week there would be a few less guys available, due to suspensions for inordinate affections.

The small number of guys who preferred girls felt they had found heaven on earth. Hot-blooded and full-bodied young women were everywhere for the taking. The rules against handholding, making out, and dating, as well as a dress code that dictated no pants for the ladies only fueled the repressed passion. And if that weren't enough, to thumb their noses at the biased and outdated policies, the sororities also secretly adopted their own dress code, which prohibited panties of any kind.

A few days into the first semester, there was a required chapel service called for men only. As the testosterone-filled group settled down a bit in the ancient auditorium, an obviously uncomfortable dean of students began a sermon against the dangers of masturbation. With cloudy eye and a struggling intellect he delivered a convoluted castigation on sexual desire.

He admonished us to pray. But when we pray, we should not pray about our sexual problems, for that will tend to keep it in our minds more than ever. We should pray for faith, our friends, and our families. And the only godly way to conquer the problem was to keep it out of our mind by not mentioning it ever—not in conversation with others, not even in our prayers.

In place of all the brisk and breezy life filling the auditorium just moments before, there was now a hopeless and dead silence. Shuffling out of the auditorium dazed and in awkward forced solitude, the message was clearer than the dean's eyes—we were not to talk to our friends, to God, or anyone else about the evil desires that raged within. The major institutions of our lives: family, church, school, and now higher education urged us to repress our deepest and most basic needs.

Nothing could unseat their strange beliefs. The recurring message from our professors was: "It's better to marry than to burn." To make matters worse, we were told there would be no sex in heaven; and they ominously warned the second coming of the Lord would happen any minute. This was not true, of course, but it made for great preaching.

The rub was that we were a good deal more than Christians; we were hot-blooded men and women. Unfortunately, in the closed system of our religion, the only godly way to have sex was to marry. So, of course, we married. And fast.

There was no such thing as pre-marriage counseling from the church or college. As long as both children (and that's what we were, children) were "good Christians" and one was male and the other female, the marriage was summarily blessed and performed. And to those whom God has joined, let no man put asunder. No matter what.

There was not only an all-out race between the gals to woo the few eligible men on campus; there was also fierce competition between both sexes for musical popularity. I hadn't ever seen anything to beat it. It's a fact that whenever in life you face a person who sings, there's always gonna be a competition.

For some reason, when it comes to musical auditions, adults are rendered mere children in their actions. Many a time I had seen a couple of boys, strangers, meet by chance, and say simultaneously, "I can beat you up," and go at it on the spot. But I had always imagined, until now, that sort of thing belonged to kids only, and was a sign and mark of childhood. But here were these religious college-age divas duking it out and taking Christian pride in it.

Having sung in the mountains all my life and never one to shrink from a competition, I put my name on the audition list for the elite choir on campus. Waiting my turn among a long line of hopefuls in the decrepit and musty hallway of the music building, for the first time I experienced the cruelty and cattiness of competing singers. It was the first of many such auditions and proved to be a learning experience of catastrophic proportions.

Confident but hushed talk of head and chest voice, singing across the break, thoughtful dynamics, and classical repertoire filled the small space. There was

65

conversation about breath tones, vocal coaches, and lifting one's soft palate. It may as well have been Greek to this ignorant redneck boy.

I can only imagine what the audition panel thought when I walked in, reared my head back, and wailed away (with a decidedly closed palate) at an old Southern Gospel song, *The Unseen Hand*. They listened politely and then asked me to match pitch with the notes played on the piano. I had no idea what they were talking about and with cold sweat breaking out all over me, I unsuccessfully tried to sound the notes with a quivering voice. The empathy that often seemed a blessing bestowed to me became a curse that day as I realized the audition panel felt sorry for me. A flush rose to my cheeks and ashamed, I quietly made my exit.

I suppose a wiser young man would have quit many times during the discouragement and loneliness of the next three years, but something deep within would just not let me. It took twenty-one failed auditions before I finally earned a bit singing part composed of seven short words. But that is for another chapter.

It's also necessary to foreshadow one more chapter in this story. The country pastor I was now working for at my first church did not think I should be going to college and getting new-fangled ideas. He began putting pressure on me to quit and put more time in at church. This and other events led to the most dismal day yet of my short life.

As long as I attended college full-time (at least seventeen hours per semester) my tuition was completely paid by the academic award. But unbeknownst to me, the scholarship ceased to pay when I dropped a few classes to work part-time and earn fuel money for the eighty-mile round trip commute from home. Before I knew it, my sophomore final exams rolled around and I received a terse summons to the finance office. It seemed I had accrued a bill of over $500. At that time, I was earning a minimum wage of $2.30 an hour working third shift at a yarn mill. My balance might as well have been a million dollars. I was informed final exams could only be taken when all debts were paid.

The next day a casual acquaintance told me he had also accrued a bill one semester and was unable to pay it. He decided to attend final exams anyway in hopes the professors did not check clearance slips. He said teachers almost never asked for the slips and sure enough, he was able to take all exams and pay off the balance before the next semester. I decided to try it.

My first exam was a Tuesday morning at 7:40 a.m. I had to get up at 4:15 a.m. in order to make the long foggy commute to Cleveland, Tennessee. With a dry mouth and thumping heart I walked in the brightly lit class and found an empty desk. As I pulled out my pencil and paper, the professor asked everyone to lay their clearance slips on the top right corner of the desk so that he could check them. With tears stinging my eyes, I slipped out of the room filled with embarrassment.

The Dean's List I had worked so hard to make that semester turned to all F's upon missing the final exams. I was put on academic probation.

My pastor jumped at this chance and told me I didn't need anything they could teach me anyhow. Our church was growing by leaps and bounds and he had lots for me to do. I reluctantly quit college. It wasn't until several years later, married and with my first child, that I was finally persuaded to return to school. A wise guide came from the unlikeliest of places.

As the youngest staff member at our church, I was always elected to transport guest preachers to and from the airport and anywhere else they needed to go. One of these many guests was the presiding president of the Southern Baptist Convention. His name was Dr. Bailey Smith and he had recently gained infamy by telling *Time* magazine that God could not hear the prayers of a Jew. Bailey had a reputation as a Type-A leader and was a famous hell-fire evangelist but for some reason, he took a shine to me.

After hearing our choir and watching me sing and lead music all week, as I drove him to the airport, he asked why I was not in college. I naively told him my pastor said he didn't think I needed it, to which Dr. Smith replied, "Hogwash. Everybody needs college. Randy, get your tail-

67

end back to school and make something of yourself. Don't be content to stay here in this little country church. I believe God has great things for you. Get yourself back and get your degree pronto."

As he exited the car at the boarding gate, he turned and gripped the windowsill and looked at me with piercing blue eyes. His unwavering stare locked onto me and he repeated in his Oklahoma accent, "Do you hear me, son? God wants you to get yourself back to college."

I wasn't quite sure if it was God or Bailey speaking, but never had anyone cared that much about my future. Especially a leader of his position. The words left a lasting impression and I could not shake them. That simple conversation with a subversive evangelist changed my life forever.

As fate would have it, four short weeks later I received a job offer from a church in faraway Stuart, Florida. The crude negotiations included going back to finish a degree at a nearby college after two years of service building their music program.

To my amazement, when I was able to begin classes in 1986, I learned my ACT scores were effective for ten years and so I received a full academic scholarship. I finally had an educated pastor who wholeheartedly supported my dream to complete a music degree and I enthusiastically resumed my studies. Unencumbered by family ties, close-minded religious beliefs, and a bigoted Southern culture, this new lease on life resulted in an ever-increasing perceptual view. It was the beginning of a rebirth, a renaissance in the life of a redneck boy finally becoming a cultured young man.

Palm Beach Atlantic was an emerging school of fine arts and had systematically recruited professors from world-renowned music schools such as the Juilliard School, Westminster Choir College, and Oberlin Conservatory.

The chairman of the music school was a former missionary to Japan and minister of music named Dr. Michael Simoneaux. His acne-scarred face was crowned by two shocks of white hair on either side of a center that was completely bald, and he had a big sudden smile that was infectious. He was a soft-spoken man with speech mannerisms much like the Japanese people he had worked with so long. His train of thought was short and his sentences even shorter. But he cared deeply for his students. And he had a special place in his heart for older students returning to school. He asked to serve as my advisor, and for the first time ever, I had someone with wisdom guiding the decisions that were to shape the rest of my life.

It is impossible to adequately describe the impact Dr. Simoneaux had on my life. It was not an easy time and he often wept empathically with me as I struggled to manage an insane schedule and maintain some semblance of family life, as well as quell my growing drive for perfectionism and perfect grades.

There were weeks at a time where I managed to grab only three hours of sleep per night. Many times I would fall asleep studying around 3 a.m. only to start over at 6 a.m. eyes stinging in the shower, once again embarking on the forty-minute commute for a 7:40 a.m. class. No grass grew under my feet.

Two years into my studies at PBA, Dr. Simoneaux asked if I would like to audition for one of a limited number of slots offered by a new vocal professor from New York. He felt it would be good for me and I followed his advice.

Lawrence Brown studied at the Juilliard School and the Cleveland Institute of Music. A great fan of Broadway musicals, he worked on the national touring productions of *Man of La Mancha* and *The King and I* as musical conductor, becoming friends with Richard Kiley and the late Yul Brynner. He also worked on many entertainment projects with his dancer-choreographer friend Ben Vargas.

Within the first week, I became his worshiper, and ours was the dearest and most perfect comradeship that ever was. From the first lesson, we had a chemistry that was magic. He placed me at the last slot on his afternoon schedule. The thirty-minute lessons would turn into hours that seemed like seconds.

Mr. Brown was sixty-two years old. He was a tall crusty man with a world of experience. After a lesson that would often be so intense it would leave us both drained, he would throw his long legs up on his desk and entertain my questions about the many photographs that adorned his office. He would regale me with stories such as finishing a late Broadway rehearsal with Yul Brynner in New York and spontaneously deciding to take the supersonic airliner *Concorde* to Paris for breakfast.

During my lessons, he would often let loose a passionate talk laced with expletives, urging me to sing from the soul. He would passionately wave his long arms while telling me if I could not sing with everything within me, then I shouldn't sing at all. His teaching style was exactly what I needed at that time in life. My previous vocal teachers had either emphasized passion or precision. Mr. Brown was the first to teach me that excellence came at the *intersection* of passion and precision. "They can not and must not be exclusive of one another," he would shout.

Often he would have me bend ninety degrees at the waist, having me lustily sing the entire lesson as his arm pressed down on my back, teaching me better breath control. He fought the other classically trained teachers for the right to include spirituals and Broadway numbers in my vocal repertoire and he finally gained grudging assent for me to perform *Deep River* at my first public recital for the music students and faculty. This decision was yet another blossom on my journey from redneck to renaissance.

I'll talk more about this moment in musical terms in the next chapter. But for now, let's just say the president of the college loved my rendition of *Deep River* and changed my academic scholarship to a presidential scholarship, which paid not only my tuition but also my travel expenses, my books, and incidentals. It was a huge deal personally and financially.

This amazing gift gave me the freedom to take classes I ordinarily would have been unable to, due to the cost of fees and books. After three years at PBA, I became a Greek exegete, learned "text without context is pretext" in hermeneutics, and studied introductory philosophy, studied piano and music theory with a Juilliard graduate, and represented the college in numerous vocal competitions and performances with the Palm Beach Symphony.

I was twenty-seven years old and my education made me feel equal to anything; I felt there wasn't any task I couldn't turn my hand to. Already, I had doubled myself in one way, I could speak and sing both redneck and renaissance and felt at ease with either situation. I was reasonably sure no one else had the uniqueness and comfort to solo with the Palm Beach Symphony at the posh beachfront Breakers Hotel one week, and sing the baritone part in a Southern Gospel quartet at a ramshackle mountain church in the Appalachians the week after.

In my dreams, I still wandered the mountains eight hundred miles away, and my reason went calling and harking all up and down the unreplying vacancies of my birthplace. But my budding consciousness was filled with new and exciting times of intense learning and deep fulfillment.

Days turned into weeks, months into years, and on a clear, comfortable, spring day, with a brilliant sun—the kind of day to make one want to live, not die—I finally walked across the stage and was conferred my Bachelor of Arts degree in music. Mom and Dad made the fourteen-hour trip to Palm Beach and it was one of the happiest days of my life.

At the ripe old age of thirty, after spending over twenty precious years in academic study, it was finally time to bloom.

71

# CHAPTER 8

# FROM THE MOUTHS OF BABES

In a world of dark coalmines and few conveniences, a novelty show gets attention. As a young boy, when I would scramble up on the rickety altar, smile real big, open my mouth wide, and "saing," even Dad's preaching became a matter of minor interest. It wields a lot of power, music does. Appalachian folk music was four chords and the truth. Real-life stuff.

Early on I learned that music caused life to boil through my veins; and a passion for showing off got worked into the composition of my being and became a part of me. If I wanted to make life bearable, all I had to do was sing. And sing I did.

73

At kindergarten graduation, I sang "Dear Jesus, Abide With Me," and Mom said I got the lyrics confused, so instead of singing, "make my life what it ought to be," I instead sang, "make my life wadded up to be." Neither of us realized the foreshadowing of that unconscious Freudian slip.

At the age of four, when most kids were just learning to be kids, I became the second-most holy personage in the church. Much was made of me.

Of course, I quickly became all the talk on the mountain. I was soon singing at every church homecoming and music gathering (mountain folk called them "saingins") around. Apparently the whole of Appalachia wanted a look at me.

The news spread that when little Randy would sing at a funeral, it gave hope for the poor weeping creatures who thought the world was coming to an end. And since dying happens regularly, especially in the mines, I was recognized and honored as the child who by his singing helped people feel better.

I was an Anointed One. Everybody at church said it. People would pray over me and implore the Lord to use me in great ways. It was said there were things very special in store for me. Great things. Holy things.

Between homecomings, saingins, and funerals, I became quite a show. Now when you consider that everybody attended these events—and not only attended, but would never dream of missing them—you can understand there was not a person in all the mountains who would not have walked a half a day to get a free meal and a sight of me.

I wore a secondhand white shirt and skinny black tie that my mom found down in the valley at the Goodwill store. I was the "preacher boy" and carried a brand-new King James Bible that was bigger than me. Little Randy was the pride of all the matrons.

The other boys all hated me because everyone said I was so good, and because their moms always "threw me up to them" so much. In my experience, boys are the same at all ages. They don't respect anything; they don't care for anything or anybody. I remember in the Bible, Elisha the

74

bald-headed prophet had bears settle up with the boys who were causing him trouble; and I so wanted to settle with the boys who tormented me, but for now, I paid them no never mind. I had more important things to do.

My notoriety spread and in all the doing, there wasn't much time for childhood trivialities. It eventually was a great burden, but of course it was at the same time compensatingly agreeable to be so celebrated and such a center of homage. I slowly adjusted to my situation and circumstances. This fame and unnatural childhood didn't cause me any trouble for a while—at least of conscious consequence.

All-day saingins with "dinner on the ground" were common occurrences among the mountain churches. These days were also called homecomings, but they never really made sense to me; I never saw anyone come home and dinner wasn't on the ground—it was always on long tables some jackleg had built out of gray crooked wood filled with knotholes and splinters. As far as I could tell, homecoming was a custom that ought to be broken up. But they kept right on.

The day would start with regular Sunday School and a worship service, followed by a "potluck" dinner. Potluck is a type of cooperative meal where everyone brings a pot of food, and there is little or no idea about who's bringing what. So whether you'll find something you like to eat is based on luck. And whether you find something *good* to eat is based on locating your mom's cooking.

Homecomings usually happened on a bright, hot summer day and heathen mountain people who never went nowhere would emerge from the woods for the spectacle. They came on foot from the coves, from the very ends of the mountains. They smelled of mold and days of solitary living. Even the Independent Baptists (who hated and avoided most folks—especially other Christians) came from over at Suck Creek.

All told it was a rambunctious crowd, especially the Hatfield clan, and very customary of the mountains and the time. These were common folk with primal spirits, innocent indecencies of language, and different views as to morals. You never saw such people.

75

Back to the food. The air would be full of the fragrances and flavors of the time, swarming with flies, bees crawling in the food, and the ground commandeered by armies of ants. Mangy dogs covered in sores and minus most of their fur would be under the table snarling and slopping up wayward scraps. The rough-hewn tables were covered by greasy red-and-white checked oilcloths; pots and pans of all shapes and sizes filled with who knows what covered the table.

Terry and I got all excited about Granny Hatfield's chocolate cake and thought it was covered in those little candy sprinkles until we ate it and realized it was thick hair from her fourteen multi-colored cats. Those savages didn't care. They gobbled it up. It just goes to show there isn't anything you can't stand if you are born and bred to it.

After the meal, everyone would cram their bloated and sweaty bodies back into the little church for the saingin. The local funeral home would make sure everybody had a paper hand fan and most of the time there was not one empty chair. A show such as this didn't happen but once or twice a year.

I will never forget one particular homecoming day. A very special guest musician happened to be with us—he was dating one of the local girls—and offered to play for me. It was obvious from his fancy velvet western suit coat and distinguished manner he wasn't from around these parts. His name was Jim Owens and was quite famous at the Cherokee Music Festival around Oldfort, Tennessee.

There was no time to rehearse but with a warm smile and soft, silky voice, he assured me it didn't matter, and even though he didn't know my song or what key it was in, he'd find me.

The congregation being fully assembled now, the church bell rang once more to warn laggards and stragglers, and then a solemn hush fell upon the church, which was broken only by the twittering and whispering of the choir in the pews on stage behind the pulpit. Usually the choir was made up of anyone who wanted to sing (which was always almost everybody) leaving only two or three people scattered out in the audience. But on

76

homecoming days the church was so packed, the choir was full up of the lucky ones who got there first.

Dad asked everyone to stand as he prayed. Since he wouldn't officially preach at a saingin, he took full advantage of his oratorical skills in front of the packed-out church with his prayer. And a good, generous prayer it was. He could keep neither his arms nor his body still and as he progressed, he pirouetted about the stage in a Pentecostal ecstasy of happiness.

Dad went into details: He pleaded for the church, and the little children of the world; for the other churches represented; for a resolution of the feud going on in the coal mines; for our mountain; for the state; for the gov'ner; for the United States; for all the churches of the United States; for Congress; for President Johnson; for the war in Vietnam; for our soldiers; for the oppressed millions groaning under the rule of Communism; for such as have not yet experienced the baptism of the Holy Ghost and with fire; for those who have not yet spoken in tongues as the Spirit gave the utterance (he meant the Independent Baptists); for the naked heathens in Africa; and closed with a fervent supplication that the music we were about to hear might find grace and favor, and be as seed sown in fertile ground, yielding, in time, a grateful harvest of good. In the name of the Father, the Son, and the Holy Ghost. Amen and amen.

There was a rustling and the congregation sat down. The singing and shouting commenced and lasted for hours. Since Dad was the host pastor and I had achieved somewhat of a celebrity status and also had the good luck of a genuine musician playing for me, I was saved for last.

It was the largest audience I had ever been in front of. For some reason that day, either the crowd or the cat hair on the chocolate cake got into my throat instead of the song. I was halfway through the first sentence of "The Unseen Hand"—a song I knew better than my own name— when my mind went blank and my heart thumped to a stop.

Seasoned pro that he was, Mr. Jim Owens vamped on the piano (in other words, kept repeating the phrase) hoping I would somehow find a way to jump back in and

77

no one would be the wiser. A pretty young lady on the front row knew the song and sympathetically started mouthing the words with her glistening ruby red lips in a highly exaggerated manner; that distracted me even more and the four hundred eyes staring at me twirled like a kaleidoscope filled with a million colors of despair.

By this time, the whole church was red-faced and suffocating with suppressed agony, and the music had come to a stand-still. All possibility of impressiveness was at an end, and neither the words to the song nor God Himself were anywhere to be found. It was a genuine relief to the whole congregation when my dad slipped up beside me, gently patted me on the head, quickly pronounced the benediction, and ended the ordeal. Sometimes there is just no satisfaction in divine service.

One of the nice older church ladies assured me afterward that if God could use Balaam's ass, He would surely see fit to use me again. I thought back just a few days earlier to when I had finished a funeral song; the ladies present had all lifted their hands and let them fall helplessly back in their laps as if as to say, "Words cannot express it—that boy's gift is too beautiful, *too* beautiful for this mortal earth."

Spiritual fame is a fleeting and fickle thing. One mistake and you are turned out to pasture like a diviner's donkey. But the show must go on.

I had already sampled the drug of the stage and experienced the euphoria of applause. I was hooked. Approval was my opiate of choice and I vowed on a stack of Bibles to never forget the words to a song again. And the rare times I did, I simply made them up, and I ministered greatly to everyone. For a while.

Just when I had fully recovered from that horrible Sunday, tragedy hit again. One minute, my voice would sound normal; the next minute, I could barely get through a sentence without it sounding out of control—high one minute, low the next, then a weird squeak. It was not a cold or a sore throat. In fact, everything felt normal—but nothing sounded right.

My voice was changing. It's one of the many unfortunate developments—I have previously mentioned acne, body hair, and wet dreams—that occur when a boy singer reaches puberty. The phrase "growth spurt" takes on a whole new meaning.

For a normal person, I suppose it's no big deal, but for a stage personality, it is devastating. I found a medical dictionary—heck, no one else was going to tell me anything —and discovered that as your larynx (and other things I won't mention in mixed company) grow, they get longer and thicker. Also your facial bones begin to grow. Cavities in the sinuses, the nose, and the back of the throat grow bigger, creating more space in the face that gives your voice more room to echo. All of these factors (and the things I'm not mentioning) were causing my voice to get deeper.

Before the growth spurt, my voice was high and kid-like. But as my bones, cartilage, unmentionables, and vocal cords grew, my voice was starting to sound like an adult. This innocent boy soprano was becoming a mature bass-baritone—in every way.

Back in the fourth grade, after Dad exacted a solemn promise that I would learn to play it, he gave me the ancient trombone he had played as a child. The finish was coming off, it was scratched up and dented, but it played just fine until a little kid accidentally knocked it from the top of the bleachers where I had left it during the third-quarter break of my first football game as a member of the marching band. It was smashed beyond repair.

I guess Dad was worried about my voice and knew something drastic had to be done, so for my fifteenth birthday he surprised me with a fancy new trombone. To this day, I don't know how Dad scraped enough money together to buy that shining instrument of salvation, but he did and I'm forever grateful.

If not for the new trombone during those two years of vocal and juvenescent hell, I would have probably given up music and be working in the coalmines. The soft purple velvet of the case interior and the smell of oil and brass provided much comfort during those trying days. I cared for it like a baby, bathing and cleaning it in the bathtub almost every day.

That insightful gift provided myriad benefits. The slide developed my ear—my pitch perception. For those of you who might not know, there are no marks on the trombone. You have to move the slide until you hear the correct note. And the exact position changes according to humidity, tuning, and temperature. For example, third position (E flat) is usually even with the bell of the instrument, but on cold days, you have to move it up about a half an inch to be in tune.

My natural proficiency on the instrument and my budding leadership abilities catapulted me to be elected as a band officer. I was slowly finding my place in the world, in spite of the living hell of adolescence.

If you'll recall, it was along about this fateful time that my friend Brad styled my hair and one of the angels who sang was Cheri Halbrooks. She heard I used to sing at church and asked me if I would kindly consider a duet with her at the upcoming Spring Follies. My head was spinning from this newfound attention from the opposite sex, but thankfully my voice had settled down. I said yes.

Cheri was a flower child who lived just down the street. With flaming red hair, long tanned legs with freckles, and a sultry alto voice, her feminine sound was like music of the spheres to my longing ear, and the perfect foil for my maturing voice. The thought of meeting her still carries me back over wide seas of memory to that vague distant time, a happy time, many decades ago.

She invited me to call on her at my leisure to arrange rehearsals. She and her sister Terri were considered two of the most beautiful girls in school. I wasted no time and went calling the very next day.

We decided to sing an old Hank Williams song, "Jambalaya," that had just been re-released by the Carpenters. We would practice for hours. The sparks of passion that flew between us were not sexual—they were musical—and we relaxed and reveled in the glow of them. The vocal match was made in heaven and our performance was lauded and talked about for days after.

This was my first experience channeling the evocative nature of the Pentecostal style of music into a collaborative sensuality for the "secular" stage. It produced an energy in me *and* in the audience that was exhilarating. Even though my consciousness had not yet caught up with my fast-moving post-pubescent maturity, my reason reckoned I had latched onto something very powerful.

Humans are created to respond to music; that is the way we are made. We don't reason where we feel, we just feel. And providentially I had been granted the God-given ability to evoke the feelings of others.

I think Billy Joel says it best: "It's nine o'clock on a Saturday, the regular crowd shuffles in. There's an old man sitting next to me, makin' love to his tonic and gin. He says, son, can you play me a memory? I'm not really sure how it goes, but its sad and its sweet and I knew it complete, when I wore a younger man's clothes. Sing us a song, you're the piano man. Sing us a song tonight. Well, we're all in the mood for a melody. And you've got us feelin' alright." [2]

I was that "piano man" through and through. I knew without a doubt I had been born for the stage. For days on end, I would fantasize about becoming a rock star.

But as fate would have it, that wasn't in the cards. My first paid gig was leading music at a Southern Baptist church and they told me I was to be called a Minister of Music. It didn't sound very rockstarish, but it did have music in the title.

---

[2] "Piano Man" lyrics copyright 1973 Joel Music. Words and music by Billy Joel.

# CHAPTER 9

# THE SHOW MUST GO ON

Working at the church part-time now provided expense money as I attended college on my scholarship. As an untrained music major, my first voice teacher assignment was the senior professor of the music department.

His name was Roosevelt Miller and his teaching gift was encouragement. He was one of the kindest and sweetest men I've ever known. Mr. Miller was a short, rounded, slightly effeminate man with wet lips and a salt-and-pepper goatee—the first Van Dyke I had ever seen. His pants were always belted high and if he had sported a full beard, he might have looked like Santa Claus.

83

Mr. Miller taught me to open my soft palate as I sang, and there was ever-so-gradual improvement under his tutelage. "Randy, my son, it's not bow-errr of roses—it is bow-eh of roses; open the back of your mouth when you sing the syllable *er*." I can hear him now. "It's like sticking a pear in your mouth, big side toward the back."

After a year of study, Mr. Miller gently told me he had taken me as far as he could go, and he recommended I change voice teachers the very next semester to the chairman of the music department. Mr. Miller would continue in my life, singing often as a guest at my church, and he was the featured soloist at my wedding.

My second voice professor, Dr. Burns, was tall, slim, and carried an air of dignity. He was well over six feet tall, in his thirties, and already had slightly graying hair. Where Roosevelt was a tenor, Dr. Burns was a bass-baritone like me. His teaching method was laid back like Mr. Miller but far more scientific. He was the only voice teacher in the music school to have earned a doctorate. He taught me the physical principles of resonance (what it means for the voice to buzz), sinus cavities, and posture. He also stressed the importance of an attractive physical appearance.

Dr. Burns was a very busy man and was often late for our lessons, but the few minutes we had together were golden. My voice and my study matured as I sang songs like "Bois Epais" ("Gloomy Woods") by Jean Baptiste Lully. It was my first piece in the French language and the Baroque style.

As my resonance deepened, people at church started saying I was like Gomer Pyle. Gomer was a television character played by Jim Nabors from 1962–1969 and introduced in the middle of the third season of *The Andy Griffith Show*. Wide-eyed and slack jawed, awestruck by the simplest of things, he had a high-pitched, squeaky hillbilly voice until he began to sing. When he opened his mouth, the country bumpkin would transform as if by magic to an operatic performer with a rich, deep baritone-bass voice.

The similarities were indeed striking and one could see how people thought it, but whenever one of those church people got a thing into their head, there was no getting it out again. I knew that, so I saved my breath, and offered no rebuttal.

Maybe there was some truth to it. I reckoned my "Gomer-esque" persona was off-putting at college too, because I could not win an audition. Inevitably, my name would be absent from the soloist list on the bulletin board with no explanation. If you recall, I would try out for over twenty solos, to no avail. It took six months into my vocal coaching under Dr. Burns before I finally snagged a one-sentence solo in a Christmas musical.

It became a blur after that. The solos kept coming and I was chosen to be student director of the one-hundred voice Campus Choir. I also earned my first spot in the prestigious music school Honors Recital.

The high point during my studies at this college came when I won an audition to play the role of Gabriel in a newfangled contemporary Christmas musical called 'Specially for Shepherds. It was totally different than anything previously attempted in the conservative religious music world.

The score was written in Broadway style by a Los Angeles avant-garde composer named Ralph Carmichael. As a successful writer, producer, and record executive, he was one of the driving forces in the creation of this radical new kind of music for the church. He was later dubbed "the father of Contemporary Christian Music."

Carmichael also wrote the iconic string arrangement to "The Christmas Song" for Nat King Cole (the arrangement we still hear today), and his resume included works with some of the biggest artists in American music history including Pat Boone, Ella Fitzgerald, Rosemary Clooney, and Bing Crosby. He composed music for popular television programs such as *I Love Lucy* and *Roy Rogers and Dale Evans*, and a long association with pianist Roger Williams also produced the million-selling musical score to *Born Free*.

The two-hundred-voice choir for 'Specially for Shepherds was chosen by area-wide auditions and was comprised of college students and the best community choir members. The entire Chattanooga Symphony

Orchestra was hired to play the score and Mr. Carmichael himself came to personally conduct the performance.

It was my first introduction to this thing called Contemporary Christian Music and to a real live professional musician (other than Jim with the velvet suit, of course). I was hooked from the get-go.

My first major role introduced me to the world of make-up, costuming, endless rehearsals, and celebrity treatment. I felt like a star. Even though I had not managed to become a rockstar, this exaltation of religious celebrities was pretty darn close—and it was both addicting and intoxicating.

The stage was now becoming my home. And it would soon become my very soul.

From the moment the first note of the symphony sounded, euphoria like I had never known swept over me. The experience transcended reality. I *became* Gabriel and together with the young lady who played Mary, we set that night to music.

No matter if you choose to call it "anointing," "flow," "charisma," "karma," or "destiny," I realized anew that night my talent and ability to communicate meaning and emotion moved people. Deeply. The empathy that for so long had been my enemy—viscerally feeling pain for the kid Leroy beat up on that East Lake junior high playground, feeling embarrassed by my failed auditions, feeling mortified by my mistakes—that night became my ally.

The lifelong battle between my instinct and my intellect, between my reason and my consciousness, had honed this empathic gift to razor sharpness and had equipped me to read the audience and then feed off their emotion. It was heady power to instinctively know how to sway the crowd at will, and the heightened emotion of the Pentecostal style of worship provided my budding empathy the perfect breeding ground.

When our bows came, it was my first time to experience a standing ovation from a crowd of thousands. I knew it would not be my last.

Like many child celebrities, the need for continual applause for my *performance* had become a gateway drug.

I had discovered the "religiously acceptable" way to medicate the existential anxiety of life. And I was damn good at it.

My blossoming talent soon led me from the redneck regions of Appalachia to the renaissance riches of Palm Beach. It was there I first understood that music gave me the power to become all things to all people. In the extreme poverty of the mountains, music was utilitarian—a shorthand of survival; in the extreme affluence of the beaches, music was the ultimate luxury—a higher revelation than religion or philosophy. Music from the soul can be understood by everyman.

It is cruel, you know, that music should be so all-encompassing. It has words of wishful thinking for the blue-collar plebian—words like strength and freedom. And it also has words of empathic reality for the white-collar aristocrat—words like loneliness and pain. Music speaks of disappointment and unrequited hope. It also speaks to the cruel irony of survival of the fittest and the everlasting beauty of monotony.

But perhaps the cruelest irony of all—for me at least—was captured by the words of T. S. Eliot in his poem, "The Dry Salvages": "music heard so deeply that it is not heard at all . . . "

In Palm Beach, music became my obsession and the need for applause consumed me. I would spend hours alone in a hot, musty, and dilapidated practice room with an old upright piano rehearsing and repeating one single melismatic (many notes sang together as one) phrase.

Hours melted into days upon endless days. I craved the opiate of approval. And my reason said that if I worked hard enough, in the heady climes of wealth, power, and white linen—fame was mine for the taking. The frenetic work soon began paying dividends.

David Sprenkle was my third vocal coach. He was a slender, nervous, complex man of indeterminable age and always on the ragged edge of apprehension. All the passion of my former college was put aside and precision became our god. My slavish addiction to approval created a model student and my empathic gifts enabled me to discern the formula for a perfect grade.

87

Gone were the days of sloughing off the pronunciation of a foreign word. We would work endlessly on French pronunciation. "Randy, form an 'e' sound in your vocal cavity, while pursing the lips into an 'o' shape." "Randy, roll the 'r,' roll the 'r.'" "Randy, work up a healthy spit when you are singing Schubert."

We would also work eternally on structure. "Randy, as a baritone soloist, you must understand that by using a melody originally in quadruple meter but starting it on the weak beat in triple meter, Gabriel Fauré displaces the strong beats and creates rhythmic ambiguity. Tension is our friend."

This emphasis on precision harkened back to Miss Sorrells' insistence for standard cursive writing. The swirls and curlicues were to be added only after the fundamentals had been mastered in such a way that they became rote. It made sense. *Perfect* sense. I worked harder.

It was about this time when the Dean of the School of Music, Dr. Simoneaux, suggested I audition for one of four coveted spots as a student of the previously mentioned adjunct professor from New York, Lawrence Brown. The previous emphasis on passion by Mr. Miller and Dr. Burns combined with the demands of precision by Mr. Sprenkle had provided the perfect foundation for my introduction to the talents and teaching skills of Mr. Brown.

Under his tutelage, the planets aligned at my first recital-seminar performance. Attendance at "rec-sem," as we called it, was mandatory every Friday afternoon. To maintain a music major status at Palm Beach Atlantic, a performance in front of the school of music was required once a semester. Everyone dreaded those eternal sixty minutes. It was one thing to perform for a large nameless, faceless audience—but quite another to stand naked in front of a jury of fifty or sixty critical peers.

Even the class virtuosos felt the pressure. I'll never forget the rec-sem performance of a marimba player who was arguably the finest music student to ever attend PBA, and who would later go on to excel at the Juilliard School. One fateful Friday, he stood up to perform and about three minutes in, he let the audience get into his head. He froze, mallets in mid-air. As we were taught, he started over only to freeze again at the exact same place. After four excruciating attempts to complete the song, he quietly placed his mallets on the keys of the marimba, lowered and shook his head, and walked off stage, eyes filled with tears. A performance was only worth a fraction of our grade, but because it was in front of our peers, it was a crucible of the highest order.

Since I was an "older" married student (at that time I was twenty-six) and a commuter, most of the students did not know me. I could not afford to pay an accompanist, so my church pianist volunteered to play for me.

To fully appreciate this story, you must know that Milda Luce was as wide as she was tall. Literally. She stood just over four feet tall and was about seventy or eighty years old. But something magical happened when she placed those short stubby fingers on the elegant keys of a piano. We became one and her presence instilled a confidence I had once only dreamed about. She had been a musical prodigy as a child and a long and satisfying career had equipped her with a mastery of myriad musical styles. She was the rare pianist who was equally at home playing "by ear" as she was playing the most difficult classical composition.

At rec-sem that day, the bored students were taking in the odd combination of four-foot-tall Milda walking in with the six-foot-tall mysterious older student. It was also their first time to formally hear a student of Mr. Brown. If that weren't enough, Dr. Claude Rhea, the president of the college (who held a doctorate in music) slipped in unannounced to the back row of the tiny seventy-five-seat auditorium.

I was slated the third performer out of six. Mr. Brown had decreed that I make my PBA college debut with the song "Deep River." He had managed to get faculty approval for the song since it was a Burleigh arrangement. Henry Thacker Burleigh helped make Negro spirituals available to classically trained artists and music schools by arranging the music in a more classical form. Mr. Brown adored this marriage of folk music with classical accompaniment.

Pressure has always enhanced my performance (except for that one homecoming) and this day was no different.

From the first note, that mundane seminar somehow transcended to a spiritual experience. It was as if the simple lyric to that song, "Deep River, my home is over Jordan. Deep River, Lord. I want to cross over into campground," suddenly became a sacred song of passage symbolizing leaving my redneck world of poverty and ignorance and crossing into a renaissance of human emotion and life.

It may have been the most powerful performance of my life.

It was so quiet in the transcendence of the moment that you could literally hear the reverberation and layers of overtones from the perfectly tuned Steinway piano. For what seemed like eternity, no one breathed, and then the room erupted in a standing ovation.

No one really knew what to do after that. The reaction was unprecedented. I don't think there had ever been a standing ovation at rec-sem before. As I fell into my seat shaking and completely spent from those four short minutes, I looked over and tears were streaming down Milda's cheeks. My life would never be the same.

The next day I was asked to be the soloist for a relatively new college event called American Free Enterprise Day. It would become a Palm Beach Atlantic University tradition and continues to this day. The day is highlighted by a medal ceremony that honors individuals whose hard work and achievement exemplify the best of the American free enterprise system. It was the third year for the ceremony and the college was honoring Theodore R. Johnson of the United Parcel Service.

Dr. Rhea requested I sing the Fred Waring arrangement of "God Bless America" and contracted the entire Palm Beach Symphony and Chorale to accompany me. The event took place at the stately new auditorium of the First Baptist Church of West Palm Beach and the room was filled to overflowing. You could cut the excitement with a knife.

Again I rose to the occasion, again with a rousing ovation. I heard later that Mr. Johnson, who was sitting on the platform in the seat of honor next to Dr. Rhea, leaned over to the president and said something like, "If that's the

90

kind of students you have here, then I want to be a part of this. That was a hell of a performance by that young man."

Mr. Johnson went on to give $14.4 million dollars to Palm Beach Atlantic and much of the scholarship money went to students like me who were from families who fail to qualify for government financial aid because they work, but whose families cannot afford to send them to college.

From that day forward, every penny of my college education was paid by an all-new Presidential scholarship. For the next three years, I represented the college at numerous Palm Beach society roundtable events at locations such as the magnificent Flagler museum and the ritzy Breakers hotel. It was a heady time for this redneck mountain kid from Tennessee. I entertained celebrities, politicians, millionaires, and the wealthiest of the wealthy.

But perhaps the greatest honor at PBA came when I was asked to help fulfill one of Mr. Brown's lifelong dreams. He wanted to conduct Handel's *Messiah* utilizing the original instrumentation. Three of the soloists (the soprano, alto, and tenor) were selected from the music college faculty, but he asked if I would be willing to sing the bass solos. It was an enormous honor and for the next six months during voice lessons, we dissected each note and melisma of Handel's oratorio.

Even members of the music faculty did not believe he could pull it off. Some of the orchestral instruments were extremely rare and priceless, but the naysayers underestimated Mr. Brown's tenacity and ability to rally Palm Beach society to the cause. As the appointed date for the performance—December 5, 1988—grew closer, so did Mr. Brown's excitement.

As we gathered that night in the basement of the original historic First Baptist Church auditorium, the anticipation was at a fever pitch. Replete in our tuxedos, Mr. Brown and I slipped to the men's room, and he asked me to kindly help adjust his tie. He asked another of his voice students, Chris Williams, to keep his car keys so they would not jangle in his pocket while he conducted.

His final words to us as we prepared to make our entrance were that he wished for no bows to be taken. He

91

wanted the end to be as Handel intended—all the glory was to go to God.

The orchestra entered first and then the choir followed by the four soloists. The stage of the ancient church was tiny and cramped and I was sitting stage left of Mr. Brown's music stand and the alto soloist was to my immediate right. We were all within a few inches of each other.

The performance had been sold out for months and reporters and cameras lined the back of the auditorium. The three television networks were represented by a logo on their respective video cameras. It was a night on the town for Palm Beach society who knew a thing or two about having a party.

As custom dictated, Mr. Brown was last to take the stage and he stumbled awkwardly as he stepped up, but quickly regained his composure, looked up, flashed his signature smile at everyone and raised his baton. When the first mournful strains of Handel's overture played by those beautiful and delicate instruments filled the timeworn auditorium, it was easy to imagine sitting there in 1742 as the masterpiece unfolded for the very first time. Mr. Brown's eyes glowed with life. It was a dream come true.

Dr. Simoneaux beautifully and artfully sang the first tenor solo and the college mass choir provided waves of sound and emotion.

It was my time.

*Okay, Randy, take a deep breath and remember Mr. Brown's meticulous instruction. Careful of diction, move the beginning a little more, big breath, long phrases, watch the conductor on the last "he appeareth"; remember the open beat in the measure after "refiner's fire"; take your time and feel the resonance up high in the nasal cavity.*

I sang it with the passion gained from my past and the precision that came from meticulous rehearsal.

With the first recitative and aria under my belt, I basked in the glow of a warm smile of approval from Mr. Brown as he prepared the chorus for the seventh movement. Mary, a young faculty member, was singing the

92

alto solos. I could feel her anticipation next to me as she readied for her first recitative.

She stood to begin and her lovely face was matched only by her beautiful voice as she sang her opening words. As I turned to watch her sing (which was not a difficult task, I might add) sing, I felt a dull thud at my feet.

The hands of death are so obvious.

All six feet of Mr. Brown lay prone before me as he futilely gasped for air. It was as if every person in the building was suddenly frozen in time. The bass violinist, whom we later learned was also an EMT, leapt to Mr. Brown's aid and immediately began administering mouth-to-mouth resuscitation, followed by frantic palpitations of his chest. Another lady, a nurse, quickly ripped aside the tie I had carefully adjusted only minutes before.

Someone yelled for an ambulance and you could sense shock settling in as loud sobs and groans punctuated the eerie quiet. We were all gently dismissed from the room by Dr. Rhea. No one said a word. It was hard to believe only five minutes before, the room had been filled with Christmas joy and glorious music.

I numbly found my way to the emergency waiting room of Good Samaritan Hospital and gathered with Dr. Simoneaux, Dr. Rhea, and a few others as we somberly waited for news. I asked Dr. Simoneaux if Mr. Brown's family had been notified, and he acknowledged there had been repeated attempts. He then took me aside and wearily told me Mr. Brown had been estranged from them for some years. It seemed the demands of his career had cost him his family.

As I walked out into the Palm Beach night, I looked up and saw the thick gray clouds swirling from off the ocean, standing out against the black sky of the night. In Florida, those clouds get so close you can almost touch them and then they just fade away. It seemed an apt metaphor.

We found out later, as I thought, that Mr. Brown had been dead before he brushed my feet. His family never came and Mr. Brown's ashes were scattered at sea. During his memorial service a few days later, as I sat there in the small audience, I recalled a gray rainy day after our voice lesson a few weeks prior. I had been sitting in my car having a snack, waiting for an evening class, as I watched his tall frame run to his Bentley. For some reason that day, I viscerally and empathically felt his loneliness.

After his death, my consciousness assumed the fetal position. I often recalled Mr. Brown telling me how proud he was of me, and that I reminded him of himself when he was young. Those words that he meant as life-giving had now become a death threat.

Every time I walked on stage, I relived his death. And I fully believed that the same death—a death on stage—was my fate. It greatly unsettled both my reason *and* my consciousness.

Dr. Simoneaux was so worried about me he arranged for the chairman of our psychiatry department to provide several sessions of therapy. As Dr. McEhlhenney and I talked about death and anxiety and my conversations with Mr. Brown, his words were like pardon to a prisoner. Somehow time began its work of healing as well.

But deep within, I questioned God for crushing a moment Mr. Brown and others had worked so hard to attain. I have a videotape of that evening but have not been able to watch it to this day. It has been almost a quarter of a century and it is still too painful to consider viewing even my solo.

As if the story could not get any more unbelievable, lightning struck from a clear sky once again. Three short years later, I shared the stage at a church in Alabama with a precious man named Milton Rosser. He was seventy-nine years young and reminded me of my granny Katherine. He was (like her) a rare senior adult who had a light and laughing disposition. But while playing his violin and singing at our Sunday morning service, he suddenly fell at my feet in mid-song, stricken by a heart attack. This time it was a choir member who was the EMT, and who leapt to his aid. But this time I knew the sound of the death rattle. It was too late. Again.

The EMT immediately began administering mouth-to-mouth resuscitation followed by frantic palpitations of his chest. Another lady, a nurse, quickly ripped open his shirt and tie.

Someone yelled for LifeFlight, and once again I sensed shock settling in as loud sobs and groans punctuated the eerie quiet. Again we were all gently dismissed from the room as no one said a word. And again it was hard to believe only five minutes before, the room had been filled with joy and glorious music.

There were no therapists in that part of southern Alabama and so a part of me withered away. There was no one in my life to salvage the few remaining microscopic atoms that were still truly me. But the show must go on.

A few short days later, while still numb, I received one of those fateful phone calls. It was a long-time acquaintance who had been dubbed the music director for the Southern Baptist Convention, which was to be held at the Hoosier Dome in Indianapolis. He asked if I would perform a solo of my choosing immediately prior to the presidential address. There was casual mention of an audience of more than thirty thousand people.

I said yes, all the while imploring God to not strike the president dead at my feet. I was surprised anyone would want to get on stage with me. Heck, I didn't want to get on stage with myself.

But I did. There *were* thirty thousand people there and I suppose history has a way of repeating itself—both the bad and the good.

I told you previously that pressure has always enhanced my performance and that day in Indianapolis was to be no different. From the first note, that contentious religious business meeting transcended to a spiritual experience. At least for a moment.

Little did I know, that hymn would became a sacred song of passage for me from leading churches filled with hundreds, to churches filled with thousands.

It may have been the second most powerful performance of my life.

It was so quiet in the transcendence of the moment that you could literally hear a pin drop in that cavernous dome. For what seemed like eternity, no one breathed, and then the arena erupted in a standing ovation.

As I fell into my seat shaking and completely spent from those four short minutes, this time tears were

95

streaming down *my* cheeks. I knew Mr. Brown was giving me a smile of approval from on high.

At the closing of that session, a line of preachers formed telling me how much they loved my performance and offering me an opportunity to join them on stage as their minister of music.

They obviously didn't know about Mr. Brown or Mr. Rosser. And I didn't tell them.

# PART II
# THE MEGA-CHURCH YEARS

# CHAPTER 10

# CHURCH #1
# (THE COUNTRY CULT)

I soon realized there was no place for me to lead music at my dad's church. An older gentleman had been directing music and waving his arms there long before we appeared on the scene, and he let everyone know he would be there long after we had left.

Through a series of events later in high school, I found myself sporadically attending a little Baptist church way out in the country. Even though where I lived was considered country by most folks, the location of this church could well be called out-country. In mountain jargon, it was "in the sticks."

There were many things about that church that appealed to me. Everything was done in a systematic way. Heck, they had what they called an *order of service*. Knowing what was about to happen next and *when* it was going to happen was of considerable comfort to a kid who had cowered helplessly behind a pew at my dad's Pentecostal church, trying to avoid the rampaging Mr. Jubal Whitener during his endless "tippee-toe" shouting spells.

I liked that it was quiet. At my dad's church, everyone prayed out loud and at the same time. The prayers would not have a starting or ending place and would often be punctuated by verbal screams, physical shouts, and interspersed with speaking in tongues as the Spirit gave the utterance. You really haven't lived until you have heard forty or fifty countrified people in a tiny, sweaty, and swaying church all screaming, shouting, and speaking at the same time in mountain jargon and tongues.

The first time I heard a prayer at the Baptist church, I didn't know what to think. The silence was so loud you could hear it. One person (always a male) would pray while everyone else stood very reverent and quiet. When he finished, everyone would then sit down and you were supposed to look on the paper you got when you came in— they also called it a bulletin—to see what was to happen next.

I liked that the service started on time and ended on time. You could set your clock to it. Seventy-five minutes from start to finish. The services at Dad's church would sometimes last for hours. They would dull me down to drowsiness and were so long and disorderly that our parents didn't seem to mind if we kids slipped in and out every once in a while to grab a breath of fresh air.

It was during one of those forays to the outside during church that these virgin lips received their first kiss. It happened behind the outhouse one damp, dark mountain night while all the adults were inside helping some sinner "pray through." I was twelve at the time and had just finished singing a solo.

100

A willowy and earthy sixteen-year-old flower child named Brenda with long, straight blonde hair and smelling of incense was visiting her step-dad. She whispered that I had a lovely voice and it was cool that I was the son of a preacher man like the song, and suggested we take a stroll out back. Ah yes, the price of fame.

Once again, I digress.

There was a significant difference between the depressing, dilapidated church buildings of Pentecostalism and the minimalistic, newly remodeled Baptist sanctuaries.

The first time I visited Church #1, I remember thinking it looked like a brick chalet. It had a white box at the front of the roof, topped with a white steeple shaped like a tall pyramid. Inside, the high A-framed ceiling was made of wooden slats embellished with four massive wooden trusses that ran from the high point of the ceiling all the way down to the floor on the sides of the church. The high-backed pews were in two sections and would seat about three hundred people.

The industrial carpet was a seventies-era burnt orange. There was a wide center aisle with two smaller aisles on each side that were made even smaller by the occasional truss. The obligatory choir loft had three pews and was flanked by two small rooms with doors—one on the side of the loft and another to the front of the auditorium.

A baptistery with a velvety green curtain was behind the choir center stage. An upright piano was on stage right and a rectangular Baldwin electronic organ was tucked behind a modesty rail on stage left. There were two steps up to the stage that doubled as altars and a massive wooden angular pulpit front and center stage. A matching communion table sat in front of the pulpit on the main floor and completed the sparse utilitarian furnishings.

There was no art of any kind, unless you count the tall flowers in vases in shadow boxes above the piano and organ.

The pastor was a tall slim creature of fifty-five with straight sandy hair. He always wore some sort of shark-skin suit with a pressed white shirt and thick tie knotted with a full Windsor, in the fashion of the day. He was extremely hyper and possessed a type-A personality. In his

101

former life, he was quick to tell you, he had been the number-one salesman for a meat company, but had decided to give up his retirement to follow the higher calling of the ministry.

He quickly learned that selling Jesus Christ to people was pretty much the same as selling ham, and the tiny country church became an overnight sensation. At least, to some. The jury was still out for some of the patriarchs and matriarchs of the region. They had seen a lot of things come and go.

This was about the time I entered the picture as a naive eighteen-year-old. The new thinking of Church #1 stood in stark contrast to the old-fashioned Pentecostal churches of my Appalachian upbringing, and proved very appealing to my growing cravings and inclinations.

Almost before I could blink, I was offered a part-time job as youth pastor and youth choir director. I accepted without a second thought. This was the summer before I was to begin my first semester at the small Pentecostal Christian college twenty miles north.

The part-time adult music director was also a music student at Tennessee Temple University in nearby Chattanooga. It was an ultra-conservative, hyper-evangelistic Baptist college. I believe the correct terminology goes something like this: independent, fundamental, pre-millennial, soul-winning, King James only, Bible-believing, Baptist college; teaching the blood, the book, and the blessed hope.

The summer before I began working at the church, I attended my last event as a high school kid at a Christian youth camp in North Carolina. The church music director was the staff representative—in fact, I was told, he had recommended the camp. That should have been my first clue.

I knew I was in trouble the moment I walked off the bus. The male counselors and campers all had buzz cuts and matching uniforms that would have made a conservative military man proud, while the girls wore long-sleeved buttoned-up blouses with shapeless knee-length culottes or long loose-fitting cotton dresses.

102

They all had plastic zombie-like smiles and blank eyes. In fundamentalism of this sort, they have ranks and castes, and a person isn't ever a person; they are only part of a person and can't ever reach their full capacity. This group looked like they had come straight out of a book I had just read called *The Stepford Wives*. It was as if I had taken a sci-fi school bus trip that had started in the present-day hippie-era of the seventies, and somewhere between Ringgold, Georgia, and Brevard, North Carolina, we had hit a time warp and wound up back in the fifties or in Stepford—or worse.

As I hesitantly walked down the steps of that old yellow bus, time stopped and everyone seemed to freeze and stare at me as if *I* were the freak. Compared to the extreme religious sub-culture I was looking at, I suppose I did look the part. My thick curly hair was grown out in the style of the day and formed into a loose afro almost a foot high. I sported a silk shirt painted with psychedelic flowers, replete with huge blousy sleeves, and my bleached skin-tight jeans with massive bellbottoms were accessorized with a pick-comb topped with a black fist sticking out of my back pocket. My size-twelve feet were shod with multi-colored three-inch platform shoes. You can imagine the shock.

What I had planned on being a fun last week as a "normal" teenager and camper at an idyllic North Carolina mountain retreat at the end of a long hot summer quickly became a living hell. Our youth group was promptly divided and assigned to separate cabins. The music director mysteriously disappeared and the cult-like counselors commenced their well-trained programming techniques.

The camp was divided into two teams of three hundred kids each and every activity earned points. The counselors treated the competition as a life-and-death struggle. To them, winning was everything and they took it very seriously. "True Christians are not sissies," they screamed with zeal. They told us we were part of a militia for God. We were in a war with Satan and his legions. We were told there were demons behind every bush. This week at The

103

Wilds was to be a training ground to exorcise our demons and better prepare us to face a sinful and evil world.

I soon learned the camp leadership was affiliated with Bob Jones University, the educational fortress of radical religious fundamentalism. Here's some of what they are purported to believe: Men are to be the authoritarian head of the home and church; women are created to submit to their husbands and have children; all abortions without exception are murder; homosexuals are perverts who disobey God; any person not white Anglo-Saxon is from an inferior race; and any other religious beliefs other than their own represent the Anti-Christ.

Each cabin was taught a military-like chant to randomly shout in the large mess hall during meals. My head was spinning. Now I felt like I was in Hitler's Berlin in the thirties. We attended a chapel service each day that was filled with repetitive fundamental religious rhetoric. Last thing at night, there was a campfire for each cabin when the counselor personally reinforced the dogma of the day to their seven impressionable charges.

At the first such campfire, we campers were given a lecture about dating. We were told that even a simple act, such as holding a girl's hand, was fornication. This was more than I could take. After only six hours, I'd had my fill and was truly pissed off that my vacation had turned into a freak-filled nightmare. Shaking my head with disgust, I snarled, "If what you are saying is true, then I'm already damned to the deepest pits of hell. So I might as well go to bed. Good night."

I stalked into the cabin and my yet-to-be-tainted cabin mates gasped in horror and disbelief. It was easy to believe my six mates were unsullied from the sins of the flesh, but I had sincere doubts that our overzealous counselor practiced what he preached. Earlier that day, I had seen him flirting to high heaven with a cute female counselor.

The anger channeled into my highly competitive spirit and I began racking up points for our team by winning the games and quickly became the de facto leader of the "Scarlet Knights" team to which I had been assigned. The camp leadership was not pleased.

104

Beating the system and earning points quickly became everything to me. I sang a solo—my standby church song, *The Unseen Hand*—in the talent competition to get 10,000 points for our team. The adult judges rejected my solo, saying it sounded too worldly and had influences of Bill Gaither.

But there was nothing they could do to swing the athletic events. My cabin won the pillow basketball tournament—10,000 points. I showed the boys how to secretly load our pillows with wet rags to make them more lethal. Our team won the big ball contest by working together as one—25,000 points. The boys of the Scarlet Knights were mopping up. But the girls on the other team, I think they were called the Blue Crusaders, were winning their games against our girls and were matching us point for point.

It came down to the last day.

Two events on that fateful Friday were worth 100,000 and 200,000 points, respectively: the "street evangelism" event and the greased watermelon contest. Both of these competitions included the boys, so we Scarlet Knights felt we had the championship in the bag. But alas, it was not to be. The leaders at this camp were not pushovers.

At the campfire on Thursday night, we were prepped for the coming big day. The greased watermelon contest (worth 100,000 points) was at the lake in the morning, followed by a bus trip to the nearby town for street evangelism (worth 200,000 points). As the counselor wrapped up his talk and proudly told us our cabin had been chosen to compete for the Scarlet Knights team in the greased watermelon contest, he paused dramatically and then told us there was one condition in order to participate in street evangelism.

He said there would be a barber and chair set up on the porch of the main lodge in the morning if anyone chose to utilize them. Certain members of our team (meaning me) had hair touching their ears and they would not be permitted to leave for street evangelism. However, if they submitted to a haircut, they would be able to represent their team and we could win the camp championship.

105

It was shades of my dad and that damn shaver from hell all over again. What is it about hair anyway? As I sat there listening, I went from somewhat pissed off to downright seething. There was a long uncomfortable quiet. I could feel my mates' eyes as they realized the entire camp championship, and all we had fought so hard for, would hinge on my decision.

I forcefully said, "I am happy to go street preaching or witnessing or evangelism or whatever the heck you call it, but there is no way under God's green earth I will sit in that barber's chair." The counselor then triumphantly replied, "Well, Randy, you realize this is not just about the camp championship; it is about poor lost souls who will go to hell because you are not willing to get your hair cut."

To which I replied, "Oh, no. I am perfectly willing to go witnessing, but *you* guys and your stupid rules and regulations won't permit it." I stood up and pointed my finger directly in his zombie eyes. "So it is *you* and this stupid camp that will have the blood of those poor lost souls on your hands. Not me."

The next day at the greased watermelon contest, with hundreds of frenetic screaming campers on each bank, even though I couldn't swim yet, it seemed that Jesus (who I recollect had long hair Himself) let me walk on water and after almost drowning the other team singlehandedly, I triumphantly slammed the greased watermelon in the opposing team's bucket.

But we were 50,000 points short. I didn't get my hair cut, and they didn't allow me to go street witnessing. Our team lost but I felt like I did the right thing somehow. Once again, however, my reason questioned my consciousness. As our music director mysteriously reappeared and the church bus pulled out that afternoon, I could see the lead counselors from both sides looking at me and shaking their head in sad defeat.

It was my first taste of cult-like religious legalism and it would not be my last.

I started my job as youth pastor the next week and under the leadership of the pastor and myself, the group exploded. We soon had over one hundred kids. The left

106

section of the pews was filled with excited teenagers on Sundays. The youth choir flourished and we planned our first tour to the mountains of West Virginia to lead Vacation Bible Schools. We designed matching outfits, took professional photographs, made posters, and performed musicals. Our church had never seen such.

A year later, our adult music director resigned and I was offered the job. At the ripe old age of nineteen, I became a full-time minister of music. My ordination soon followed.

The adult choir flourished and we soon had over fifty singers. We also designed matching outfits and were the featured singers for our many revival meetings. I was naive enough to think we could pull off one of the new-fangled "worldly" Bill Gaither Christmas musicals we had performed at college. It was called *His Love Reaching*. We bought the reel-to-reel accompaniment track, rented a player, customized and spliced the tape with a razor blade at a local radio station, and rented a disco ball.

Little did I realize it would be the first of twenty-nine Christmas musicals I would direct over the next three decades at the five churches I served. It was a smashing success. The little country church and choir grew and soon became the talk of our Southern Baptist denomination. We were even invited to be the featured choir at a famous Bible Conference in far away Little Rock, Arkansas, with the contemporary group Truth and a popular Southern Baptist blind soloist named Ken Medema.

This invitation happened because Bill Stafford, a famous traveling evangelist, had purchased a country home near our church and started attending the rare times he was home. He loved music and enthusiastically bragged about his church and our choir everywhere he went. His circle of friends included all the famous evangelists of the day and he had them come and preach revival meetings for our church.

Once again, I became a novelty. These Baptist luminaries were not used to the passionate singing of a Pentecostal kid. Their universities and seminaries taught an emotionless and expressionless singing style that supposedly separated a Christian soloist from the world.

107

Our resident traveling evangelist loved my youthful passion and invited me to travel with him several times a year. He told me he would pay all my expenses and give me a $500 honorarium. He also bought me several fancy new suits crafted by Hart Shaffner Marx.

Before I knew it, this twenty-two-year-old redneck kid from the Appalachians was boarding a Delta Airlines flight —the first of my life—en route to Oklahoma. The evangelist was a wonderful and fun traveling companion, and I learned a lot. But I quickly realized the life of a traveling revivalist required ultra hype and afforded only short-term relationships with the hosts. You would just get to know someone after seven days and then you were up and saying goodbye. I preferred building long-term relationships with the people in my home church.

It also became clear I was a homebody. I would lay on my sterile hotel bed for hours lonely while looking at photos of my young wife and brand-new baby girl. The life of a traveling evangelist is much like that of a touring band. While the "stars" are on stage basking in all the adulation and glory, someone has to be at home cleaning the toilets. It quickly became clear I was not cut out for the life of a "roadie" and my wife was not content to just stay at home barefooted and pregnant.

But that time with evangelist "Wild Bill," as he was called, was a training ground that proved invaluable later on. He taught me how to socialize and introduced me to all sorts of fascinating people. He was always quick to include me in conversations and at meals and was a consummate gentleman.

The evening services were typical revival hours and I did my job, but I was mesmerized by the lunch Bible studies he would teach for a small group of businessmen each day. I had never heard such thoughtful and fascinating teaching. I would quiz him all the way home about the authors he had mentioned and dialogue endlessly about the topics.

But after the three or four revivals per year, it was back to the life of a church staff member.

Our pastor (the former ham salesman) was a master at raising money and had no hesitation preaching about it at every opportunity. Our resident traveling evangelist also specialized in fund-raising and the combination of their expertise mixed with the growing legalism that permeated our church proved a fertile breeding ground for extraordinary tithes and offerings. Paying penance is a sure-fire way to cure the guilt of sin. And when almost everything is a sin—a church budget is gonna soar.

We gave the first evangelist, who was a friend of Evangelist Bill, a $3,000 love offering. He took his money and reeled away drunk with fortune. In those days, in the mid-seventies, a revival meeting started on Sunday morning and climaxed the following Sunday—and three grand was a truckload of money, especially for a country church of around three hundred souls. At each of the nine services, Pastor would get up and take the offering. And boy, could he take an offering.

It was a sight to see. He would begin, straight off, in the most innocently artful, transparent, and skillful way, to lead up to the subject of stewardship. The salesman in him had no qualms at all about shaming everyone into giving their last penny, and his close was a sight to behold. When he had finished, he smiled all around with the satisfaction of a god who is doing a handsome and gracious thing, and is quite well aware of it.

The offering plates in that little blue-collar country church would be filled to overflowing every night.

Well, the word spread on the preaching circuit that our little church in the country was good for a powerful love offering—not to mention photo ops and bragging rights for who could get the *biggest* offering—and every famous evangelist scrambled to adjust their busy schedule and come preach a revival for us.

Our pastor thrived on it. I'm not sure what *he* was making off all this, but the church was his life and he figured it should be that way for everybody, so we would have eight to ten revivals per year. When you add musicals, Vacation Bible Schools, special events, youth nights, and assorted other services, it didn't leave time for much else.

It was understood that a good church member would work overtime to earn extra money to give to the church and would attend every church service. It was the Christian

109

thing to do. It became one's life. And we were told from the pulpit if it wasn't our very heartbeat, there was probably sin in our life. There were also frequent hints that we should be wary of other churches.

Several things happened that began to open my young and very naive eyes.

Excessive pride in one's church, almost to the point of fanaticism, is one thing taught by cult-like churches. I bought in just like everyone else and invited my two closest friends from high school to church. Staff members were required to evangelize and even though my friends attended First Baptist Church in town, as far as our pastor and many of our evangelists believed, that didn't give them a "get in to heaven free" card.

Colleen, one year my junior at school, was the first person to beat my ACT score. She and her boyfriend Clint were two of the classiest and intelligent people I had ever met and I desperately wanted them to see my work at church. Clint had been the marching band captain and both were excellent musicians. Colleen would go on to become a gastroenterologist and Clint earned his doctorate in music and is a university music professor and also a virtuoso on the tenor saxophone. We all shared a love for contemporary music and had frequently attended concerts together before my time at Church #1.

As I proudly showed them around before church, Colleen noticed a bulletin board filled with photographs. I had completely forgotten about the board and would have never taken them close if I had remembered the contents. Her face was filled with hurt and confusion, and a tear streamed down her cheek.

On the board were pictures of a special youth service where our pastor had urged us to burn our evil rock-and-roll records. As a leader and staff member, I was required to lead by example. Even though I had begrudgingly participated, that hesitancy was not captured in the photo Colleen had seen. It portrayed me throwing an album by *Chicago* into a roaring fire.

It was the exact album that Clint and Colleen had given me as a Christmas present during high school. We were in awe of the musical excellence and instrumental stylings of

110

this relatively new band, and they became our standard of excellence as aspiring musicians.

I didn't know what to say—I was mortified. I blushed so hard I could feel that cursed bonfire of the vanities burning my skin. This proud moment with my dearest friends had disintegrated into a cauldron of flames. After a few awkward moments, they somberly excused themselves, saying they didn't think they would stay for church.

That night as I lay awake in bed, I realized something was not quite right. The teachings of my church seemed fine as long as we sequestered ourselves in our "sanctuary," but they did not seem to stand up as well in the light of the real world.

The second thing that triggered my consciousness happened a few months later. Dr. Bailey Smith, the President of the Southern Baptist convention and pastor of a mega-church in Oklahoma (mentioned previously in chapter 7), was scheduled to lead a revival at our church. Our Pastor had been growing steadily more eccentric and dictatorial in his leadership style with our growing fame and success. We were slowly philosophically parting ways.

He loved hair-brained promotions and sales tactics. For instance, he once created what he called a "dollar box" and placed them at each exit of the church. The crude wooden boxes had a slot on top and a cheap cassette tape recorder inside with his tinny-sounding voice saying, "Don't dare to pass without putting a dollar in the box for missions." He truly was out for our last dollar—all in the name of God, of course. The ends always justified the means.

Pastor decided the revival theme was to be "We're God's Army." The decree came down at staff meeting that I was to teach the choir a military chant he had written especially for us. I was to lead them down the center aisle and then around the entire church, while calling the chant as they repeated after me. I was to shout out, "We're God's army, yes we are." Then the choir was to repeat. You know the drill.

It did not sit well with me. By this time, I was twenty-three years old and even though I was a late bloomer, I had finally started thinking for myself a bit. I tried to reason

111

with the pastor. I pleaded, reminding him that Dr. Smith was the president of the entire fourteen million members of the Southern Baptist denomination. He was also the pastor of a very large and influential mega-church and had an earned doctorate in theology. Surely, he did not want us to come across as country hicks. I suggested we try something else.

The more I implored him, the more adamant he became. I realized there was no changing his mind so I gave up. As the revival drew closer, my reason told me I worked for the pastor and it was my job to lead the chant. But my consciousness just would not let me. It did not make sense. It was embarrassing and my job as a staff member was not to brown-nose but to keep my church and my pastor from looking like fools.

I decided to refuse to lead it.

You should understand no one ever disagreed with the pastor. Especially his paid staff. He was the Lord's anointed and you should never "touch the Lord's anointed." He was the undisputed authority. A dictator for Jesus.

He was flabbergasted. At first, he didn't know what to say. Then he steadily began to get mad. He told me that it was not my job to think for myself. I was paid to do this, but if I wouldn't—he would have our associate pastor lead the chant.

As I sat there watching the amused surprise on Dr. Smith's face as the choir entered chanting, and looking at the choir's faces as they saw their leader sitting there, I realized there was something really wrong with this picture. It was a cult-like atmosphere, and even though most of the choir would do anything the pastor asked, I wasn't buying it.

That was really the beginning of the end. You may remember Pastor had already demanded I quit college; this fateful revival week was also when Dr. Smith told me at the airport to get my butt back in school and make something of myself.

Things started happening pretty fast after that. Pastor was worried about my influence but his cult-like leadership style demanded the strictest loyalty and unflinching obedience from his followers.

To make matters worse, we were also parting ways theologically. One Sunday, he preached a message and blatantly said that God did not want us to pray for sinners. The point he was trying to make was that we should go out and witness to them, but this was not a philosophical question any longer. He was treading on heresy and completely twisting the context of scripture. I confronted him with verses about intercessory prayer, but he would not recant.

A plethora of popular evangelists of the day were coming through our church, including Moody Adams, Bill and Anabel Gillham, Sonny Holland, Sam Cathey, Peter Lord, Manley Beasley, Ron Dunn, Freddie Gage, Paul Jackson, James Robison, Bill Stafford, and many more. There was no filter to help us process these teachings. Some were vastly different from our pastor's preaching and many contradicted each other. But Pastor just got up afterwards and smiled with no clarification whatsoever.

We would watch manipulative and cheesy movies like *Burning Hell*, and the next month we would watch the heady film series *How Should We Then Live* by Dr. Francis and Edith Schaeffer. One evangelist would expound on the total depravity of man and champion Calvinism, and another would teach that we are all saints and champion Arminianism.

The books my evangelist friend, Bill, had recommended were not helping matters. Tomes such as *The Idea of the Holy* by German theologian Rudolf Otto, *Turkeys and Eagles* by Peter Lord, and *Letters from a Devastated Christian* by Gene Edwards were causing me to think in ways that were not acceptable to my pastor's beliefs.

It was a confusing time theologically, but a lot of what I was reading was slowly making sense in helping resolve the many questions of my Pentecostal upbringing. I was growing up and spreading my wings, and it did not fly well in a church built on manipulation and control.

A few days after the Bailey Smith "God's Army" revival, Pastor left a note on my office door requesting my presence in his office immediately upon arrival. Ordering me to grab my coat, we jumped in his truck and headed to the construction site of our new church. Due to our fast growth, Pastor had decided to relocate the one-hundred-year-old community church about ten miles closer to the city.

Walking the perimeter of the new property, he firmly told me that my allegiance needed to be single, focused on the church. As the new father of my first child, I had also realized our family was never at home. We were spending every waking hour at the church. I mentioned hearing another minister preach that our priorities were to be God first, family second, and church third. He stopped cold in his tracks and turned to look me straight in the eye.

"Get this straight, Randy. The priorities are God first, church second, and family third. That's what the Bible teaches and what we will practice as long as I'm the pastor here." I knew it was useless to respond, and I knew at that moment I was leaving.

To lighten the mood a bit, I must tell you one last story about Church #1. It's about a thermometer.

Somehow Pastor had gotten another flamboyant scheme in his head to build a large thermometer to track the progress of giving to the new church building. He wanted the increments to be big enough to show significant progress for each $100 given. As he diagrammed it in staff meeting, it became clear it was going to be humongous. In fact, when the associate pastor and I went to measure the front of the church where Pastor wanted it, we realized it would reach from the floor to the highest point in the ceiling. This would necessitate placing it in the very center of the stage, blocking a large portion of the choir.

Because of my aptitude for drawing, I had been designated the church artist. So it was the associate pastor's job to build it and mine to draw and paint it. When I was taken to the back parking lot to see the assembled thermometer, I was stunned by the size of it. At the scale Pastor wanted it, it would literally cover up three-fourths of the choir and dominate the stage. And it was to remain there for months until we raised the money.

That was simply unacceptable to me. I asked the associate pastor to wait a moment; I would be right back.

Assuming I had gone to secure pencils and paints, he was shocked to see a saw in my hand. "Randy, what are you doing? Randy, you know you can't cut this. Randy, please, please don't cut it . . . there will be hell to pay. Pastor will be furious! Randy, surely, you're not going to cut it. Oh my. Oh my! Randy, please, for the love of God, don't cut it!"

I knew as I wielded the saw and cut it in half, I was cutting not only the unsightly thermometer, but my career as minister of music at Church #1 as well.

Pastor was furious! I was verbally and formally reprimanded and a note was put in my personnel file. My years of success with the music program were the only thing that kept me from being fired on the spot. After seven long years of continually dealing with an authoritarian leader who only wanted a yes-man, I had had enough.

On the plus side, I had learned self-discipline, punctuality, and how to work hard. But unfortunately the negatives far outweighed the positives.

A few days later, my phone rang and a man named Mr. Lloyd Campbell asked me to lunch at the fanciest restaurant in nearby Chattanooga. He treated me to a lavish meal at The Town and Country restaurant and said he had a job offer for me. It seems he had attended one of our many revival services and had been impressed with my solo and our choir.

His son, L. C., was the pastor of a new church in Stuart, Florida, and was looking for a minister of music. Both Mr. Campbell and L. C. were musicians—in fact, L. C. had a Bachelor's degree in music from Oklahoma Baptist University—and placed a high value on both higher education and great music. Mr. Campbell felt he would be willing to let me go back and finish college. It would be what he called a win-win.

It was like music of the spheres to my weary ears.

115

# CHAPTER 11

# CHURCH #2
# (THE CREATIVE CRUCIBLE)

I slipped out of bed, padded barefoot to the eleventh-floor balcony, and soaked in the coral greens and myriad shades of blue highlighting the vast expanse of the Atlantic Ocean. A soft breeze gently rippled through my curls and the rhythmic thundering of the surf wafted in and out, followed by echoes and crashes. The moist heat beneath my feet was accented by the distinct smell and taste of salt. I could hear a pleasant rustling of palm fronds, as fluffy clouds tinged with pink and gray hovered over the water's surface—so close I could almost touch them.

I felt emotion rising deep from my consciousness to the upper reaches of my reason. I was in heaven. Or at least the closest I had ever been. It dawned on me that, like my grandfather, I must have "sand in my shoes."

Church #2 had put me up in this South Florida condo in order to woo me. It was working. This quaint little beach town just north of the Palm Beaches was easily the most perfect place I'd ever been. I could see why Mr. Campbell's son moved here from Chattanooga, never to return.

Pastor L. C. Campbell Jr. is the only pastor I worked with that I will mention by name. He was (and is) slightly short, pleasantly chubby, and delightfully witty. He is ten years older than me almost to the day, and at age thirty-four, already had slightly graying hair at his temples. If I were to describe him in renaissance redneck terms—he was like a banty rooster, replete with all the latest gadgets.

The day we first met he was wearing earthy cotton—beige khaki slacks and a forest green pinpoint oxford shirt —with perfectly shined burgundy penny loafers and no socks. He smelled of exquisite cologne. I learned later he had concocted his own personal mixture of three fragrances that was redolent of Calvin Klein's *Obsession for Men*, which came on the market a couple of years later. He had a Montblanc "writing instrument" in his front pocket, Wayfarer Ray-Ban sunglasses in a cool Havana color hanging from a Croakie eyewear retainer, and drove a brand-new Toyota Maxima that matched his sunglasses.

After an hour of frenetic conversation while sweeping from one picturesque place to another, we ended up at Church #2. I had never seen such a place. As we walked up the wide cedar ramp to the building, cloistered by huge palmettos and palm trees, L. C. proudly told me they had carefully preserved the distinct natural floral state and respected the habitat of the fauna. He pointed out the plethora of cute little Florida scrub lizards.

One member of the building team was a landscape architect who designed golf courses, another owned a high-end construction firm, and another was a geologist. The grounds and building looked like pictures I had seen of posh island resorts.

I was not in the Appalachians anymore.

The inside was cozy and had a pleasing aroma. I settled into it and instantly felt at home. White cedar was chosen for the interior building materials and furnishings because in Africa and India, the White Cedar tree has been known for centuries as "the tree that heals." I first heard the word *aromatherapy* that day. I learned that fragrance was beneficial and balancing, soothing, normalizing, calming, relaxing, as well as healing. It was to be the first of many new words and concepts L. C. would teach this mountain hick.

Of course, L. C. had the latest and greatest sound reinforcement system and wasted no time urging me to the stage to "audition." The warmth of the speakers and the acoustics of the building provided the ideal environment in which to sing. I felt the now-deep resonance of my baritone voice literally permeate the room. I knew by the look on his face that I would be offered the job, and I knew by the thumping of my heart that I would take it.

For the next six years, he would have me on that cushy stage at every opportunity showing off for someone. Pastor L. C. has always been one of my greatest supporters. Several years later—long after I had left Church #2—when I was asked to sing at the Southern Baptist Convention at the Hoosier Dome in Indianapolis, it was he who graciously and eloquently provided my introduction.

As L. C. and his wife Gail courted my young wife and I, we sashayed to the opulence and beauty of Jupiter Island, admired the coral reefs of Bathtub Beach, and ogled at the gold watering bowls for dogs on Worth Avenue in Palm Beach.

We also got real sunburned to prove to the folks back home we had been to the beach, and ate the first fresh seafood of our lives. In fact, it was the first fish this landlocked sierra boy had *ever* consumed. My head and my palate were spinning. I liked it all. The more exotic it was, the better.

Then I swaggered back to the Appalachian Mountains and announced we were moving to the southern parts of Florida. To the beach, no less. Not only was I the first person in my family to graduate high school, now I was the first person to move a "far piece" from home.

But leaving Tennessee was harder than I thought. My young wife and I were in our early twenties with a sixteen-month-old little girl. She was the first grandchild on my in-

119

laws side of the family and it was a very emotional departure. As I drove down Interstate 75, my mind raced with excitement and possibilities but sobs and tears filled the other side of that vehicle the entire trip. We would never return to live in the mountains of Tennessee again.

Being first at things seems grand and glorious when you are a young man, but as the years passed, I realized that most "pioneers" are destined to be lonely souls. I suppose the people of the renaissance would label that loneliness avant-garde and existential, but the folks back on the mountain would just say I'd forgotten where I had come from. As I grew older (and hopefully wiser), I found there was some truth in both.

It was obvious from the git-go that we were not in the South any longer. The Treasure Coast of Florida may be geographically located in the South, but I soon found why there is usually an epithet in front of Yankee. All the wooing, sashaying, and touchy-feely stuff from the previous visit got pulled right off me the moment my young wife, daughter, and I wearily pulled the big rental truck into the parking lot of our rental quadruplex after sixteen long hours of driving.

An old man with a big nose came running, shaking his fists, and screaming cuss words in what seemed a foreign dialect. I learned later he was from New Jersey. It seemed that he called himself the %$&# president of something called the %$&# HOA, and didn't I know that %$&# trucks were not permitted in the %$&# parking lots?

Except for a few dog-drunk coal miners, I had never witnessed anyone acting and speaking in that manner, especially in front of womenfolk. He raised my redneck ire. After a few choice words in my Southern dialect explaining the virtues of being a gentleman, I was too tired to fool with him any longer. I turned to my task at hand and ignored him. He was obviously not one to let common sense get in the way of black-and-white thinking. There was no way to unload the truck into our apartment without temporarily pulling into the parking lot. Even an uneducated redneck would know that. He finally walked away grumbling and cussing under his breath.

I was *definitely* not in the Appalachians anymore.

120

South Florida often seemed like a dystopian dumping ground for senior adults like this bored old man. The Interstate 95 corridor runs from Maine to Miami, disgorging millions of "snowbirds" escaping the cold and gray Northeast for the balmy southern coasts of the sunshine state. As Miami and Ft. Lauderdale became overpopulated and increasingly crime-ridden, Vero Beach, Jupiter, and Stuart became the destination of choice for those more affluent.

After a few months of playing golf every day, they quickly grow apathetic and the useful ones start new businesses, while the useless ones generally live to cause trouble in anyway possible. The phrase "get a life" never seems more appropriate than in Florida neighborhoods, roadways, and unfortunately, in the churches. The millions of senior adults who have fled to Florida deciding to waste away in "retirement" are an untapped source of wisdom that, if channeled properly, could change the world for the better.

Looking back, even though I was commuting and finishing my degree, singing for the college, and working at the church full-time, the six years I spent at Church #2 were easily the happiest of my ministry. It was the only church I served in those thirty years that was actually able to not only preach love, but practice it; to not only teach cross-generational community, but live it; to not only accept grace, but extend it.

My perceptual view was forever changed. Every tenet of my former life was challenged. The ways I worked, played, and lived in the past were being affected by completely new ways of doing things; ways that the controlled legalism of my childhood, adolescent, and early adulthood would not have tolerated. My reason was freaking out but my budding consciousness was screaming with pleasure.

Moving to the opulence and excess of South Florida from the poverty and simplicity of the Appalachians alone would have greatly altered my perception of reality. But add working with a pastor who was not afraid to think for himself and think deeply; and attending a more liberal college where most of the professors hailed from the

121

Northeast, all resulted in a volatile mixture of challenging growth.

I soon learned that perception is a tug of war between the attempts of culture to impose truth on us, and our efforts to transform this truth into our being. In other words, I learned the self is formed by integrating elements of the conscious *and* unconscious mind. It is where the conscious and unconscious—or to what I've been referring throughout this book as consciousness and reason—clash *and* where they balance each other that forms our perception.

This kind of stuff is not something you "chew the fat" on around the porch of the old country store outside of Beersheba (pronounced 'bir-shē-buh), Tennessee. I was beginning to grasp that the incessant battle between my reason and my consciousness was a *good* thing, a healthy thing, and perhaps the only way to stay unstuck throughout life. In fact, the very definition of perception is understanding by means of the senses *and* of the mind.

Increasing one's perceptual view can also be painful. Every day for five years, I endured people laughing and making fun of my pronounced Southern accent; especially pseudo-intellectuals from the Northeast. Because of their own limited perceptual view, many Northerners automatically stereotype anyone with a Southern accent as slow of mind and dense in understanding.

I was somehow able to take the ridicule in stride and it was an effective change agent. Aided by my voice lessons at college, my soft palate began to lift and my tongue began to enunciate. Dialect is a double-edged sword. When I would travel home, everyone thought I was "taking on airs." Sometimes you just can't win. I'm convinced that's why many people never do what it takes to change for the better. It's just too hard.

I've learned, however, there's usually good with the bad. Northern people just don't have the filter that Southern people have. That leads to derision but it also makes for refreshing and sometimes hilarious honesty. I found out quickly you don't say stuff you don't mean, like Southerners are prone to do. If you tell a Yankee to "come on over and see me some time," they are likely to show up at your doorstep the very next night. They bring new meaning to "what you see is what you get."

One of the senior adult ladies who helped regularly at church was captivated by my singing and surprisingly by my Southern accent. Her name was Anna and she was Norwegian, but had lived most of her adult life in New York. Her accent was delightfully thick and let's just say she had aged well. She was around seventy years old, stunningly beautiful, almost six feet tall, and statuesque—with the most gorgeous blue eyes I've ever seen.

She also had a pronounced limp from a dancing injury, and along with the physical toll of growing older, she felt her attractiveness had been greatly diminished. She lamented this to her lady friends one day as the staff was hosting a luncheon for our volunteers. I happened to be sitting at the table next to her and the natural encourager in me turned before I knew it and said, "Baloney, Anna, you are still as beautiful as ever. I've never seen eyes like yours. They are captivating and they literally sparkle like diamonds."

There was a pause and then everyone burst into laughter. I had no idea what *faux pas* I had committed, but I was foolish enough to ask. In her charming accent, Anna said, "Randy, no one *ever* looks at my eyes." I honestly had no idea what she meant. She placed her long slender fingers underneath her firm ample bosoms and lifted provocatively. "These forty-two double D's are what men look at. They never see my eyes." I could feel my face flushing as I stumbled for a response.

She and her friends gleefully went on to tell me she had sustained her leg injury during a career as a burlesque dancer. She reached for her purse and proudly whipped out a tattered black-and-white photo to show me. The women in those magazines I found in Papa's back room as a young boy had nothing on her.

Those ladies teased me mercilessly about Anna's "eyes" from that day forward. At my going away party, when I left Church #2, she held me close weeping and whispered that I was the first man, except for her husband George, to

123

compliment her eyes and mean it. She told me in that charming accent she would forever adore me for *seeing* her instead of just looking at her.

I understood what she meant. I obviously didn't have her show-stopping body but my stage persona and singing voice seemed to always be what people admired about me.

Under my naive leadership, the music program at that creative little church somehow grew and prospered. The adult choir attracted graduates of the prestigious Oberlin music school who had relocated to the Palm Beaches, singers from the *Voices of Liberty* from Epcot at close-by Disney, and even former movie stars. It was the day of adjudicated choir festivals hosted by our denomination, and we won straight Superiors at every opportunity.

Under the influence of Mr. Brown, my vocal teacher at Palm Beach Atlantic, we created our own Broadway-style Christmas musicals. They were a huge hit in the sophisticated society of the Treasure Coast. We became the talk of the town and every performance sold out.

The Covenant Choir, as the adult choir was called, was also tapped to present numerous national premieres of the latest musicals for leading choral companies at national conferences for musicians.

The youth choir was equally talented. This developed from a collaborative relationship with Ron Corbin, the local award-winning high school show choir director. His choir, OPUS, at Martin County High School, was a perennial all-state winner in a very competitive Florida school system.

Ron and I loved the idea that his best singers would keep their singing and dancing chops up during summer break in my choir, so he enthusiastically became our feeder system. We bought an old city bus, named it "Barnabus," and hit the road. The church youth choir would perform summer musicals with full choreography on the road for national tours in places like Washington, D.C., and we also traveled back to the impoverished churches of the Appalachian Mountains.

On these summer tours, I was the choir director, tour manager, chaperone, and bus driver all rolled into one. We would cram thirty high school kids into that old diesel city bus and drive for thousands of miles during the summer. It is a miracle that any of us survived.

It was the day before commercial drivers license requirements for bus drivers and even though I had no business driving a bus full of teenagers, because our church was small and our budget tight, that's exactly what I did. Somehow it was in my head that since we were doing God's work, we were invincible—sort of like superheroes.

One summer on tour, while driving the narrow, twisting mountain roads of the Appalachians, a coal truck suddenly appeared, careening almost out of control around a narrow curve on the edge of the mountain. I was going up the mountain on the sheer side of the road and there were no guardrails. The truck operators were used to having those mountain roads to themselves and drove them like racecar drivers. That trucker was certainly not expecting to come face-to-face with a broad and awkward city bus taking up his road, and his suddenly shock-filled wide eyes will be forever branded into my consciousness.

I swerved dangerously close to the right edge on a non-existent shoulder and could sense the gravel rattle down the sheer cliff road. He jerked his steering wheel to the right and scraped the mountain wall. I thought we had survived until I heard the screech of metal as the back left edge of his truck sliced the side of our bus like butter. A window exploded above one of the kids who was reclined against it napping. And just like that, it was over.

At the very next shoulder, I eased over to the side of the road and made sure everyone was okay. I then pulled the big silver handle, opened the hydraulic door, and stumbled down the steps shaking like a leaf. I walked to the other side of the road, out of sight behind a tree, and got violently sick. Realizing full well what might have happened, I gathered myself and assessed the damage to the bus, duct-taped the window with cardboard, and resumed the trip. Still trembling at the wheel, this unschooled greenhorn thanked God for miraculously sparing us to do His work.

Ten years later, as the on-call pastor at Church #4, I stood over the cold steel operating table of a hospital emergency room, looking at the already stiffening corpse of a fifteen-year-old member of our youth group. She had just been killed by a car during a church high school outing, while trying to cross a busy Florida highway to purchase a soft drink. The youth pastor had denied her request to attempt the crossing, but she waited until his back was turned and tried it anyway.

The odd thought occurred to me then that just as God does not preside over football games, he also does not offer the promise of protection at church events. While waiting for her parents to arrive to console them when they first saw her mangled body, for the first time in my life, I questioned God.

But as an innocent twenty-something late bloomer at Church #2, the harsh reality of life had not yet visited me, and I truly thought I was invincible.

There was a growing restlessness in me. After nearly six years at Church #2 and as my college education was nearing completion, I became more and more disenchanted with Pastor L. C.'s leadership style. His laissez-faire approach and the relatively slow growth of the church did not satiate my growing lust for changing the world.

My callow youthfulness and the growing influence of a new and subversive elder of the church who took a shine to me created an unfortunate series of events. One of my biggest faults has always been giving people my heart before ensuring it could be entrusted to them. I've told you previously it made me feel good when people liked me.

This new member of our church was a business owner in Ft. Lauderdale and had recently moved his family north to Stuart to escape the overcrowding and growing crime. He prided himself in his similarities to the actor Clint Eastwood and was accustomed to getting his way. He had previously been a deacon and leader at a mega-church in Ft. Lauderdale and idolized the pastor there.

That pastor could not have been more opposite of L. C. He was tall, perpetually tanned, wore custom-tailored Armani suits, Bali shoes, and was a silky-tongued orator. He was also ambitious and driven to become the appointed leader of his denomination. His church was one of the fastest growing in America.

Our small church and Pastor L. C. just couldn't compare to the good ole' days of this man's former church and pastor there in Ft. Lauderdale. This man befriended me and would often treat me to lavish lunches and dinners. The attention felt good and I was entranced by his stories of the mega-church down south. His disillusionment in our church and in Pastor L. C. began to soak into my skin.

He took me down to Ft. Lauderdale to introduce me to his former Pastor and to show me around the mammoth church. He subtly told me he believed I had the talent to one day lead a music program at a church like this. A few nights later, I dreamed of standing on stage at a huge new church leading worship in front of thousands of people.

Unlike most dreams, this one would not go away. It recurred with growing frequency and every detail of that dream church was etched into my mind. My growing discontentment led me to call Pastor L. C. in front of the elder board and complain about his lack of organization and leadership.

I will never forget that meeting. The surprise and hurt was written all over L. C.'s countenance and he never said one word in his defense. But neither did the new elder who had influenced me with his contagion of an idealized past. After the meeting I felt used and dirty. It is one of the few moments in my thirty years of ministry of which I am ashamed.

That same man had also encouraged me several times to make a recording to sell at the occasional revival meetings I was still doing with the traveling evangelist. It seemed like a logical idea and I approached a long-time producer friend in Tennessee to coordinate the project. He hired the Nashville String Machine and a prominent Nashville producer do the vocal, brass, and string arrangements. It was a wonderful project. But to this day, I don't know how I was intending to pay for it. I just didn't take into account that all the musicians would need to be paid *before* I could sell enough to pay them.

It was my first attempt at entrepreneurship and it was a catastrophic lesson. I went to the man who had influenced me to make the recording and hesitantly asked for a loan to pay all the bills, promising to pay him back incrementally

127

as I sold the album. I will never forget what happened next. He looked at me with suddenly cold steely eyes and informed me that he didn't give *anyone* loans—not even his family. This was not about friendship—it was about business.

I was stunned. The album had been his idea all along. The harsh realization that he may not be what he seemed hit me like a ton of bricks. I had no idea what course of action to take.

At dinner that night, I painfully recounted the story to Chuck Clark, a new friend who lived next door in our quadruplex and attended our church. Without a moment's hesitation he asked how much was needed to pay all the bills. I hesitantly told him and he promptly went over to a safe and took out enough one hundred dollar bills to pay for everything.

For the second time that day, I was stunned. I had never seen that much cash. And I had no idea how he came by that much money. As far as I knew, we were both struggling to make ends meet. Heck, we shared meals to save money.

He firmly told me that it was not a loan—it was a gift, and if I could pay it back someday, fine. And if not, that would be fine too. He told me he believed in me and the album, and he was glad to do it.

A few months later, Chuck also helped me get a second car for my wife to drive while I was away from home for endless hours at work and at college. He was a comptroller at a local Buick dealership and taught me a valuable life lesson that I still practice today called the A-B principle.

He asked me to drop by the dealership and he showed me an old but clean canary yellow Mercury Zephyr. He told me he was selling it to me—not giving it to me—and that I owed him $1,200 for the car. I was told I had to promise to pay him $100 for twelve months and because I was a friend he would not charge me interest.

The only stipulation was that after twelve months, I was to continue to put that same amount into an automobile savings account each month and drive the car until the "wheels came off." He showed me on paper how interest paid for a depreciating car mounted up over time and said that if I would listen to him, I would never have to pay a car payment again.

I drove that Mercury Zephyr until the top was rusting out. When it would rain, the floorboard would fill with water and the cloth ceiling would fall and billow around my head.

That car lasted for six years and I was able to sell it for $900. Chuck's A-B principle dictates that a car should never cost the owner more than $2,000 a year. Somehow I have adhered to that formula and have made money on every car I've owned since that time.

I had found a true friend and this redneck kid learned some hard life lessons. How I wish my story could say that I was careful whom I trusted from that moment forward. But alas, I continued to give my heart out at will and the wounding continued. Fortunately more men like Chuck came across my path.

One Sunday at Church #2, an older gentleman approached me as I came off stage at the end of service and asked if he could have the honor of a lunch appointment. Relatively new to our congregation, it was easy to see he was a no-nonsense but very classy kind of guy.

At lunch, Mr. Robert E. (Bob) Slater introduced himself as a new church attendee and after instructing me to dispense with my Southern hospitality and all this formal Mr. Slater stuff, asked if I would be willing to accompany him to the new maximum security prison once a month to sing. He wanted to mentor and encourage prisoners, saying he had learned through experience that music was the ideal cultural bridge for the varied personalities who found themselves incarcerated.

His no-nonsense Bostonian personality became warm and engaging as he talked about his calling to minister to these men who had made huge mistakes. He believed that despite their heinous sins, they had potential to return to freedom and contribute as healthy members of society.

I was convinced and by the end of our lunch agreed to help, even though I was too busy at the time. I've found though the years there are certain moments in time that an intuitive response can change the course of one's path in life-altering ways. Unfortunately, most people can't or

129

won't listen to their intuition (their consciousness) and they miss some of life's greatest opportunities.

Thankfully, for some reason, my consciousness overruled my reason and common sense on this decision and the consequences changed my life forever. Mr. Slater became the first wise guide of my life.

His story began to unfold as we made our commute to the prison each month. Before he had taken early retirement to South Florida at the age of forty-nine, he was elected the youngest-ever chief executive officer of John Hancock Life Insurance Company. He helped make architectural history with the innovative but workable John Hancock Tower in Boston, and served as chairman of Boston's branch of the Urban Coalition, an organization that sought to enlist big business in the war on urban poverty.

After an early retirement, he returned to school to earn a doctorate in criminal justice to be able to mentor prisoners more effectively and learn the ins-and-outs of the correctional system. He firmly believed thorough preparation was required in order to make any significant difference in culture.

The first meeting Bob and I had with the wary but savvy warden of Martin Correctional Institution was like a college education for me. The warden quickly realized that Mr. Slater was no ordinary Joe and that the prison was lucky to have someone of his reputation and influence. We were granted unprecedented access to the highly fortified prison. We were even allowed to bring the Covenant Choir there to present our Broadway-style Christmas musical one year.

Because I had agreed to help Bob before I knew anything about his resume, he determined to mentor me as well as the prisoners. He sent me to numerous high-level business classes and helped me understand the vital importance of thoroughly assessing my leadership skills. He helped me understand my strengths and challenged me to do great things.

After a few months of work at the prison together, he instructed me to choose a high-quality piano for the church and to let him know the cost. We purchased an exquisite

Yamaha Grand for Milda. You may remember she was the little four-foot high virtuoso church pianist who played for my college recitals. She was beside herself with joy and in the clouds for months.

But even more important to me was Bob explaining afterwards that he and his wife Roberta had a fund set aside for gifts such as this when they felt prompted to make a donation to a worthy charity. This was an entirely new concept for an Appalachian kid who had only known hand-to-mouth living. I had never owned a home, was in debt, and didn't even have a savings account. Bob assured me that one day I would be able to emulate his charitable giving and he urged me not to forget it.

The church was paying me just over twenty thousand dollars a year. Now with a family of four, the exorbitant cost of living in a resort town, and struggling to finish a Bachelor's degree, never in my wildest dreams did I think his prediction would ever come true. But sixteen years later, it did. Ah, I'm getting ahead of myself.

One evening in late 1989, still at Church #2, I received another of those fateful phone calls. It was a job offer for a much larger church in Southern Alabama. I listened for a moment and then said a gracious "No, thank you." I explained that after years of work, I was only one semester from college graduation at Palm Beach Atlantic and it would be impossible for me to consider moving at this time.

The pastor wouldn't take no for an answer and called several more times with more lucrative financial packages, while saying he felt I was the perfect person for the job. I continued to say no. Finally, they offered to fly me back and forth between Mobile and Palm Beach each Monday through Thursday, for the entire semester, so that I could finish my degree. They had also worked to incorporate all rehearsals and staff meetings around the weekend when I would be there.

It felt good to be wanted so badly. And it seemed sexy and cosmopolitan to fly back and forth for five months. I think I also bought into the Western ideal that bigger is better. Our little church in Stuart was not growing very fast and this church in Alabama was seemingly exploding. The pastor was highly driven, seemed more like the mega-church pastor in Ft. Lauderdale, and was a distinct contrast to L. C.'s laid-back style. So without a lot of further thought, I gave a tentative yes.

Church #2 and L. C. had taught me so much. I had learned how to think creatively, how to evaluate and understand people's internal thinking, the ability to comfortably work with people of influence and power, how to understand and utilize my own unique leadership styles, my first lessons in money management, and so much more. The church had been true to their word in letting me go back to college and had supported my education. My second daughter had been born there. In many ways, it had become home.

But for some reason, it wasn't enough. I wanted more. I didn't really know why; it just seemed to make sense in the grand scheme of things. I truly believed I had been called to change the world. And it just didn't seem like my calling could come to fruition in Stuart.

So I turned in my resignation, watched for the first time as a professional moving company packed up our belongings, said goodbye to one of the most beautiful and desirable places on earth, and headed north on the Florida turnpike, back to the confines of the South.

# CHAPTER 12

# CHURCH #3
# (THE COMMUNITY CLIQUE)

The South had not changed—but I had. I immediately found myself unpleasantly affected by close-minded innuendos and sociological prejudices that would have seemed proper and airy graces of thought at an earlier period of my life.

When people are born and brought up under that redneck sort of arrangement, they never find out for themselves that there is a world outside their limited perception, and they don't believe it when somebody else tries to tell them different. Within six weeks, I knew I had made a huge mistake by moving back to the close-minded stubbornness of the Bible Belt.

133

I wanted to change the world (especially the religious part, which seemed so hurtful), so I determined to invent, contrive, create, and reorganize things; set brain and hand to work, and get started. Staying busy was the least of my problems the first five months. The weekly commute back to South Florida was mind-numbing and exhausting. It was winter and I quickly experienced the frustration of canceled flights, weather delays, sleepless nights on the hard benches of Atlanta-Hartsfield International Airport, the frustration of flying stand-by, and the vital importance of a savvy travel agent.

My college curriculum included two very difficult senior-level classes—Music History and Music Composition—and in my negotiations with Church #3, I had neglected to require them to provide a place to stay each week in West Palm Beach. The dubious solution to this dilemma leads me to my next story.

Four classmates from the School of Music had an inner-city shotgun rental apartment. They lived in the left side of an ancient duplex with a living room that opened to a bedroom crammed with four bunk beds, which, in turn, led to a tiny kitchen and then to a combination bath and laundry room crudely encompassed by four extension rods that served as closets. They generously offered to let me sleep on the couch in the living room for a nominal fee.

To help you understand the location of our apartment, the next summer I happened to see a Showtime special exposing the worst crack houses in West Palm Beach. As the camera panned the neighborhood, I realized they were showing the very apartment that had served as my home for five months. The neighborhood was condemned, flattened, and razed by bulldozers two years later.

However, it was only two blocks from the college and a short drive to the airport. Safe rental options in that area were non-existent, and so at the age of thirty-two and after eight years of marriage with two school-aged children, during the week I found myself living with four single music students in their late teens and early twenties. It was challenging, to say the least.

Three of them were dating regularly and being good Christians, they courted their ladies on the couch in the

134

living room. That couch was also my bed. It was usually well after 1 a.m. when I could occupy the now-sweaty couch and try to eek out a few hours of sleep before my 7:40 a.m. class. I also had to fight the mosquitoes that entered through a gaping hole in the aging windows (there were no screens). They incessantly buzzed around my ears.

The guys were poor college students but managed to pool their resources to buy a tiny (but very loud) used window air-conditioning unit. However, it was so small it would only cool the bedroom, so they closed their door to prevent it from freezing up, leaving me out in the Florida heat and humidity.

The apartment was filthy. The kitchen reeked of dirty sink water and dishes were caked with decomposing food. The bathroom had black stuff oozing up from the cracks in the dingy linoleum and dripping off the ceiling. The toilet regularly backed up and kept the rotting wood wet, moldy, and crappy. When I had to go pee at night and would slip through the closed door, tiptoeing through the bedroom and trying not to wake the guys up, my feet would slip and slide on the greasy kitchen floor and I could hear huge rats scurry helter-skelter in the dark. I don't know if the kitchen or bathroom were ever cleaned.

One Saturday night while I was thankfully in Alabama, one of the guys woke up to see a cross-dressed transvestite crawling across the floor like a spider. He had a handful of stuff in his hands. He had slipped through the broken window in the front room and was sliding in and out under the noisy cover of the air-conditioner, gathering a pile of the guys' belongings in the front yard.

Steven was a cowboy from Texas and before anyone else could wake up, he screamed bloody murder, yanked a gun from under his pillow, grabbed his hat, and took off after the thief in hot pursuit. As the other guys stumbled out to the front yard in their underwear, they heard a gunshot and a yell. They just knew he had shot the culprit in cold blood. A few minutes later, Steven came ambling back with a big grin and every one of their belongings.

As they told me the story the following Monday, they vividly described a half-naked Steven, clad in underwear and his cowboy hat, chasing a transvestite through the inner-city neighborhood while trying to shoot him. Or should I say her? Somehow the thief escaped with its life and everyone thought it was the funniest thing ever. But that night, lying on the couch next to the hole in the window, it didn't seem as funny. It took me several nights before I finally found the comfort of sleep.

The boys courting on my bed until the wee hours of the morning, in addition to being away from family, afforded me countless hours to study. I managed to get a key and twenty-four hour access to the newfangled computer room in the music department and my grades were perfect that semester.

The geographical and sociological contrast between the Palm Beaches and lower Alabama could not have been more stark. During the week, even though my apartment was deplorable, I was immersed in the throes of a healthy and stimulating learning environment; but on weekends I found myself trapped in a dysfunctional and stifling Southern Baptist church.

The second weekend at Church #3, I was asked to travel with the pastor and the chairman of the deacon board to some sort of Baptist event in Jackson, Mississippi. During the journey I listened from the back seat aghast as these religious rednecks traded racial jokes. It was the first of many times afterwards that I realized being associated with most religious people made me feel dirty.

That region of Southern Alabama was the most depressed and unhealthy place I had lived since my childhood. The countless chemical plants belched their sulphuric poison into the rivers and creeks and there was a constant stench of rotten eggs permeating the atmosphere. It was a toxic environment in more ways than one.

One of my many pastoral duties was hospital visitation. The medical facilities were filled with cancer-ravaged patients. The wards looked like sci-fi movies and everyone I met had a zombie-like hopelessness about their yellowed skin. It was at Church #3 I realized I was not cut out for hospital visitation. My empathy sucked the patients' despair into my soul and their pain began to slowly wither away my being.

To combat the growing depression I felt each week during my on-call days, I would visit the maternity wards, put my nose against the window, look at all the little faces, and try to breathe in their new life.

Most of the people at that predominantly blue-collar church worked "shift work" at the chemical plants. Shift work meant schedules such as working four consecutive twelve-hour days starting at seven in the morning, followed by three days off, then five twelve-hour days starting at seven in the evening, followed by two days off.

The similarities to coal mining were striking. They worked long, grueling hours in a toxic environment and rarely had time for themselves. It was expected that upon graduation from high school, the kids started in the plants like their parents. The shift-workers I came to know grew old before their time. The premature aging and hopelessness of the vicious cycle of life in that community turned nubile twenty and thirty-somethings into wizened old men and women.

Another correlation was the clan-like community. Just as in the Appalachians, if you were an outsider, no matter how long you lived in the community, you were always an outsider. I never felt at home there. It was a surreal three years where I always found myself looking at my existence there with a temporary mindset.

It was into this environment that I naively approached my first major task as minister of music. I've mentioned my penchant for Broadway-style Christmas productions. In order to pull off these extensive musicals while also managing college studies, I had hired a young theatre major at Palm Beach Atlantic to assist me the previous two years at Church #2.

Because my final semester of college with the demanding class load and travel schedule did not culminate in time for adequate preparation—these musicals took almost a year to prepare—I decided to bring the young man in to help stage Church #3's first attempt at a theatrical Christmas production. It did not occur to me that he might not fit in as well in these redneck climes.

He was a creative genius and we had always worked together well in South Florida. The actors and musicians at

Church #2 loved him and treated him with a delightful mixture of respect and awe. He ate it up.

But returning to Alabama from Palm Beach for the weekend rehearsals after the choir's weekday rehearsals with him, I overheard derogatory phrases such as "he doesn't play for the same team as we do," "he's weird and different," and "he's as queer as a three-dollar bill." I could feel dissension in the air.

The disdainful hostile environment, combined with my graduation, gave me the opportunity to be more hands-on than in the past. This created multiple problems for my new leadership at Church #3.

First, I felt the undercurrent of the choir's dissension and disdain. It was the polar opposite of the choir's respect and awe at Church #2. Second, where his over-the-top personality and flamboyant style fit perfectly in South Florida, it stuck out like a sore thumb in redneck Alabama. Third, because I had more time to be creative after graduation, I had more hands-on ideas to contribute to the production planning.

All of these dynamics came together for one of the most unforgettable experiences of my career.

Two rehearsals before opening night, with the cast of hundreds assembled throughout the auditorium, many details of the production were still unclear to the actors and musicians and frankly, to me as well. My "dramatic assistant" had kept everything under wraps under the license of creative freedom. But I was beginning to suspect he was actually flying by the seat of his pants, and his lack of planning was creating a major crisis.

I could viscerally feel the restlessness of the people scattered about the auditorium, some who had been sitting for hours. Many of them had worked third shift and sacrificed their sleep in order to participate in the musical. There was no rehearsal schedule so the entire cast was forced to wait as my assistant capered about. Around 9 p.m. I finally had had enough.

Moving from my secondary position of support, I stood up and shouted, "everyone take five." I then laid hands on my assistant and asked for a word privately. In a terse but gracious manner, I reiterated my newness to this community and to this job, my empathy for all the people sitting around for hours, and my sense of urgency to understand the goals of this production. In short, I expressed my deep concern about the possibility of success two days hence.

I'd never previously had an occasion to assess the length of his fuse, but apparently it was short and I had lit it. His face turned bright red and he exploded, screaming at me and anyone who had the misfortune of being in close proximity. We watched in disbelief as he gathered toolbox, scissors, random bolts of cloth and his precious sewing kit, and then stalked out of the church, filling the sacred air with expletives.

As his bigger-than-life personality and screams still hauntingly echoed throughout the building, so did the Christmas musical. Nothing was on paper—every stage design, lighting cue, dance step, music order, and direction left with him. Reams of shimmering silver-and-gold cloth hung limply from the walls and ceiling awaiting his design and final touch.

It was as if the world slowly ground to a halt. I felt a surreal moment of hopeless despair and then I got mad as hell. As I started to run out the door in hot pursuit, aiming to thrash his prima-donna behind, a teammate I had brought with me from South Florida grabbed me, took me to the side, looked me straight in the eyes, and under his breath said desperately, "Randy, think. You can't go out there as mad as you are. How would it look? Think about your job. Think about your career. Randy, do you hear me?"

His words instantly calmed me down and thankfully I realized he was right. I collapsed into a pew, not knowing what to do next. I could feel the hundreds of people in the auditorium waiting with bated breath for what I would do next. The responsibility of leadership felt like a noose around my neck, choking the life from me.

A prim and confident lady who was married to the son of the matriarch of the church (otherwise known as the organist) slipped down beside me. "Randy," she said in a warm but firm voice, "we can do this. I've had worlds of experience in television production and I've coordinated

139

musical theatre. If you will let me, I'm happy to gather the troops and I think you will be quite surprised to see what we're made of. We don't need some outsider to come in and show us the ropes. Give us a chance."

I looked into the comfort of her big compassionate brown eyes, realized she meant it, and sheepishly and tearfully nodded in the affirmative. They did indeed surprise me, and if they were honest, they probably surprised themselves. We pulled it off together and it was a fox-hole sort of experience that bonded me with that choir forever.

After the dust had settled, Christmas was past, and I had given much thought to the matter, I publicly apologized to the choir and expressed my deep gratitude for a job well done. Pardon the cliché, but it truly was a team effort. I learned several invaluable lessons that have stood me in good stead to this day.

It is wise to determine the compatibility of the creative leadership team and the artists. It is wise to demand a schedule in writing during pre-planning. It is wise to storyboard the complete production and gain affirmation from crucial players before the first rehearsal. It is wise to stagger rehearsals so that only the people needed are present. Emotional quotient (EQ) trumps intelligence quotient (IQ) and even creative quotient (CQ) every time.

For the life of me, I do not know how the pastor who hired me was called to minister at this salt-of-the-earth bedroom community church. I had not only returned to the Bible Belt redneck South, but I had acquired another type-A retired salesman as a boss. It was déjà vu.

He was a tall, slender man with thick slicked-down black hair that formed a V on his forehead and he had coal-black eyes and brows. His lily-white skin was a startling contrast, giving him the appearance of an adult Eddie from the television show *The Munsters*. He had a tenuous and insecure smile and always seemed nervous. His fingernails were chewed to the quick.

He was socially awkward as well. He once approached a famous religious stage personality at a conference to say hello and without thinking blurted out, "I've never really liked you until today." The man (another type-A

140

personality) just stared at him like he was an idiot. Pastor came back to where he and I were sitting and recounted what had taken place, all the while, muttering prayers of forgiveness to the Lord for being such a "retard," as he called it.

His preaching style was in the manner of a television evangelist. He stalked the stage with his long strides and waving arms. He would suddenly ask people to pray and as he entreated God, he would wave both arms over his head to catch the audio technician's eye and feverishly gesture thumbs heavenward to turn up the stage monitors. It was impossible to get the stage volume loud enough for him during his message. He wanted the reverb of a giant hall to accent his phrases.

Two and a half years into my three-year tenure there, Pastor traveled westward to California for a hyper-Pentecostal John Wimber conference that emphasized laughing in the Spirit and other spiritual outbursts such as barking like a dog. As an outsider (coming from the adjacent community), he was already viewed as different by much of the congregation, and when he returned to this hundred-year-old southern Baptist church with this new revelation and anointing, it was more than they could take.

To put this community church in perspective, they had not allowed blacks to be baptized until the late eighties. One of the deacons and revered patriarchs was a proud member of the Ku Klux Klan. They had built a literal concrete fortress (it was an approved bomb shelter) to house a "Christian" school in order to educate and protect their white children during segregation. This church epitomized the word southern in *Southern Baptist* denomination. They were not a people to be reckoned with.

One Easter Sunday, Pastor got tired of everyone (including me and the two other pastors on his staff) advising him not to preach about what happened in California—the animal noises and such—but rather take some time to consider the ramifications. It was our second Sunday in a brand-new state-of-the-art 1,200-seat auditorium. I will spare you the sordid details of his one-horse leadership in the building of that sanctuary.

141

Suffice it to say, Pastor chose everything right down to the light fixtures, type of carpet, and even the color palettes. The building program lasted two long years and everyone was just happy to get it over with. The church folk were tired of being guilted into giving money every week and the staff members were tired of constantly defending the pastor. By the time it was finished, the general contractor was on the third and fourth round of sub-contractors. All the rest had walked off the job.

It was into this environment that Pastor stepped into the pulpit that fateful Sunday. He began his emotional soliloquy by describing publicly for the first time what he had seen and witnessed in California. He declared it to be of God and, therefore, the new direction of the church. What happened next was another one of those dreadful moments that caused my ministry wounds. He instructed everyone who was for him and the will of God and this new direction of the church to stand up and show their approval. A heavy quiet settled over that new monument of a building and about half the church hesitantly stood up.

It was a heartbreaking sight. One brother was standing up and another was sitting down. It was like a religious Civil War enactment. In one fell swoop, he had divided the church in two.

It was a thoughtless and immature act that would eventually bring on a lawsuit that revoked his unapproved changes—he had set the church up as a sole proprietorship —to the hundred-year-old church by-laws and constitution. The legal action returned the church deacons to power and led to his immediate dismissal.

As I wearily pulled into my driveway after the service, a wonderful and gentle family had followed me and tearfully asked me what had just happened. Tired of constantly defending my pastor, I simply said, "I'm not sure what happened. You should go and ask the pastor. He is the only one who can tell you."

Fortunately for me, only a few weeks later, the phone rang with the invitation to sing at the Southern Baptist Convention in Indianapolis and afterwards I received numerous job offers.

But this chapter closes with another bittersweet story. One Saturday, as I was putzing around the house, I noticed a car continually rounding the circular road in our neighborhood. The driver appeared to be a member of our orchestra and it concerned me a bit because he was a very unusual man and his mood swings were legendary. I instructed my girls not to answer the door and sure enough, a few moments later, the back doorbell rang.

I cautiously opened the door and it was immediately obvious something was seriously wrong. His hands were covered in blood and he was mumbling incoherently. As he collapsed in my arms, I screamed for my wife to call an ambulance, realizing he was either suffering a seizure or had overdosed. Instinctively it seemed vital to keep him awake, so for the next fifteen or twenty minutes, I shook and slapped him into a semblance of consciousness.

I also kept asking him questions, trying to keep him awake by talking. I gradually managed to understand that he had been in a fight with his wife, had hit her and felt guilty, and swallowed a bottle of medicine. Emergency vehicles and law enforcement soon swarmed my driveway and neighborhood. Our quiet suburban Alabama neighborhood turned out in droves for the show. Nothing like this had ever happened.

As the EMTs began their work, I noticed several church members among the police officers and recounted what I had learned. They asked if I would accompany them to find the wife and be there for her. Of course, I did and thankfully when we reached their house, it was the glass in the front door that had been shattered and not she who had caused all the blood.

Once the police determined she was okay, it was somehow left for me to drive her to the emergency room. I asked her to show me the empty bottle so that we could take it. He had swallowed a full container of extra-strength Tylenol. I was somewhat relieved that it was not something stronger until I learned later at the hospital that an acetaminophen overdose is one of the most deadly forms of suicide.

Arriving at the hospital, we were immediately escorted back to an emergency room with a steel table, trauma

143

nurses everywhere, and doctors huddled and working all around his body, furiously pumping out the contents of his stomach. To this day, I do not know why they just let us go in while all that was taking place. As we entered the room, his wife passed out and crumpled into my arms. I handed one of the doctors the Tylenol bottle and he said, "Holy shit." They began working even more furiously.

We were told later that I had saved his life by keeping him awake those crucial fifteen or twenty minutes and that the EMTs had lost him twice on the trip to the hospital. There is much more to this story—including me begging the wife's brother not to go ahead and finish the botched suicide job once the husband got back home. I saved the guy's life at least twice.

I've told you before I'm not a quitter, and against my better judgment, I stayed while trying to help the deteriorating situation. Fast forward three months later and I was unexpectedly called in to be reprimanded by my pastor in front of witnesses. As I walked in, I realized it was this same guy from my orchestra. He was pissed that I had never asked him to do an offertory solo on his instrument and had complained and called me before the pastor.

Only in the ministry. I had saved the guy's life from an overdose, talked his brother-in-law into not killing him for beating up his sister, and visited him every day for two weeks in the psych ward afterwards—in Alabama, anyone who attempts suicide is remanded to a padded cell in a hospital psych ward and given an evaluation.

The guy then tattled on me and called me in front of the pastor like a little kid. And worse, the pastor let him. Like I said before, sometimes there is just no explaining the human race. I've come to realize Pastor was immature and untrained. I really believe he meant well; he just did not possess a lick of common sense.

You may remember the scene from chapter 9 where Mr. Rosser died on Sunday next to me on stage, while singing a solo and playing his violin. This was the same church. What you do not know was that as the EMTs were rolling his body down the aisle, I and the other two staff members were physically restraining Pastor backstage. He wanted to go out and resume the church service.

He had not gotten to preach yet and felt he could capitalize on the beloved Mr. Rosser's death so that more people would be "saved" that day. Two of us had to continue controlling him as our executive pastor quickly went out and thoughtfully dismissed the service. Pastor was furious with us for weeks.

On the positive side at Church #3, I was able to build and purchase my first house. Because we did a lot of the work ourselves, it sold for a significant profit a few months later when I resigned, and the sale (and the generosity of our real estate agent there) provided equity for our next home purchase.

Also, while at that church, the executive pastor had insisted, against my wishes, that I donate a minimum of ten percent into a retirement fund. I was so young (age thirty-three) and felt I needed every spare penny to live. But he was right. It turned out to be one of the best things anyone has ever done for me.

The choir was very talented and had a rich legacy long before I came. It grew even more and we were able to do several wonderful musicals and events during those three short years, despite the pastor's insanity. The youth choir also flourished. People in that cliquish community somehow recognized my similar upbringing and gradually accepted me and my family while we were there through numerous acts of kindness; our children were even treated as their own. It was there I was able to finish my college degree.

But it soon became evident all hell was about to break loose, so after entertaining several job offers (including one close to home in Chattanooga), we decided to return to Florida. Yep, to Florida. I told you I had "sand in my shoes."

145

# CHAPTER 13

# CHURCH #4
# (THE EARLY YEARS: THE CORPORATE
# COMPLEX)

It was an immense place, rather corporate, and full of architectural contrasts.

It was very, very lofty; so lofty that the lights and girders way up there floated in a sort of twilight. There was an odd choir loft and stage at one end, and a balcony high up with pews at the other end. The floor was of bluish industrial carpet and the front half had three rows of the longest cushioned pews I had ever seen. The back half was filled with round tables, each with eight chairs rather battered by age and use, but all in good repair.

147

As to ornament, there wasn't much, strictly speaking; though on the stage were two flags—American and Christian.

Along the walls were a series of doors, one side leading to a large exit hallway to the outside, and on the other side were doors leading to a huge industrial kitchen and to a hallway with a dividing wall that provided privacy for what was called an "executive dining room."

In the front and center of this multi-purpose room (the back was used for a regular dining room) was a pulpit big enough to camp in; with its projecting sides and front decorated with wooden crosses. It had the look of a crenellated parapet. It was lifted high above all else. At first I thought this design was to emulate the cathedrals of the past, which were never to have a building taller than they— only to learn it was to elevate the pastor, who was short in stature, above the people.

It sat alone on an eight-foot-square riser above the rest of the stage and building. I learned later the facilities department had lovingly dubbed it "the hump." It was also forbidden to move the hump, for fear of damage. Moving either the pulpit or the hump required special dispensation from the pastor.

The outside walls were a combination of glass bricks, windows, and stucco. At that time, it was painted a cerulean blue. There was also a massive class building (what was called an educational building), with a large *porte cochere* on the east side for vehicles to offload their passengers during bad weather. Another large building housed a private Christian school that educated all twelve grades, a football field complete with bleachers, and several retention ponds.

All told the campus sat on over seventy acres located on the main road from Tampa, only 2.4 miles from the beach. It was like its own city. You could even register to vote there.

I first met the pastor at the Southern Baptist Convention in Indianapolis after I had finished my solo. If you had told me then that he pastored a mega-church like I've just described, I would have laughed in your face. One

148

would think he pastored some tiny country church out in the sticks.

He was a well-kept but stocky and short man who stood very erect. He was balding and had a voice that always sounded hoarse—as if he were talking though his nose—and had a distinct and very thick southern Arkansas accent, even though he had lived in Florida and pastored Church #4 for over twenty years.

After the first two years of his pastorate, he went through a divorce, managed to survive it without losing his job, and soon thereafter married a woman fourteen years his junior. He was ostracized by his fellow pastors in the area and by his denomination.

Pastor had clearly suffered much and he had clearly survived much. But that kind of suffering never really leaves you. It becomes a part of you, like a second skin that you can never shed no matter how much you want to. But somehow he managed to plug along and each year the church grew little by little.

When I arrived on the scene twenty years later, that little church of two hundred in backwoods Pinellas County had grown exponentially to over six-thousand members, and during that time, the smallest Florida county geographically had become the most densely populated.

The church had managed to thrive but the divorce and subsequent ostracizing had taken its toll on the pastor. He was one of the most black-and-white humans I've ever known and openly acknowledged he was a lone ranger. I believe his trust in humanity had been removed during those early years.

He was never without a gun except in the pulpit and he had trained a security team for the church that would have made the FBI proud. If a staff member made a mistake entering the passcode on the church's sophisticated alarm system, they would be staring down the long barrel of a Glock wielded by a member of the local police force.

Even though I stood as partner with him on stage for seven years and arguably had the most access to him, I never once entered his home. Except for rare trips to Montana—Pastor headed up a committee to assist the struggling churches in that state and would sometimes ask

149

me to accompany him—our relationship (as with everyone) was strictly business.

He ran the church like a well-oiled machine. His old-timey and extremely conservative management skills, complemented by a down-home and highly charismatic stage persona, provided the perfect combination for unprecedented church growth during those three decades of explosive population surges along the beaches of the Treasure Coast. Interstate 95 had dumped white-collar snowbirds from the Northeast to Church #2 in the Palm Beaches; but in this area it was Interstate 75 dumping blue-collar retirees from the South and Midwest. They were the perfect "customers" for this corporation.

Pastor's favorite saying was: "The main thing is to keep the main thing the main thing." Maybe I had been tainted by my artsy years in Palm Beach, but in all my years there, I never really figured out what that mantra meant.

My wife and I were invited down to interview with the personnel committee in the fall of 1993. From the outset, we thought we were being given some sort of weird test. Far from the beautiful beachfront condo we were provided when interviewing for Church #2, here we were housed in a dilapidated motel across the street from the new Hilton.

The room reeked of body odor and cigarettes; the sink and bathtub were clogged with standing water, and the bed collapsed in the middle. If we had not been so desperate to get away from the laughing and barking pastor in south Alabama, we would not have unpacked our luggage in that filthy room. To make matters worse, our meeting and interview with the personnel committee took place across the street on the deck of the posh beachfront Hilton— giving the impression we were staying there.

All in the name of saving a buck. I found out later that a church member owned the flea-bag hotel and no one even cared to check and make sure it was acceptable. We were still so young and star-struck, we never said a word. Unfortunately, that cheap motel room was a harbinger of the way things would be.

My head was soon spinning. During the personnel interview I was told there would be a full background and financial check, and was quizzed about my thoughts on contemporary music, my marriage, and my work habits. I was required to sign agreements saying I would never drink alcoholic beverages of any kind, never view an R-rated movie, never speak in tongues (that was the easiest one, sorry Dad), always pay tithes to the church of at least 10% of my gross salary, and that my children would attend the Christian school owned and operated by the church.

The salary package seemed substantial upon presentation by the human resources director. But when all the benefits and tithes were removed, it was only a few hundred dollars more than the much smaller church in south Alabama.

From a music staff consisting of one volunteer who helped with the choral library in Alabama, I suddenly found myself supervising a paid staff consisting of a personal secretary, a full-time media coordinator, a part-time orchestra director, and several other part-time positions—including a pianist and organist. The transition from working solo to team leader had begun.

The secretary had been passed around the office pool by several of the pastors and had not worked out for any of them. It was soon obvious that one of my first tasks was firing the secretary and finding a capable executive assistant who knew something about music. The human resources person helped a little with verbiage, but I quickly realized her main job was to keep the church out of legal liability. It was my job to do the firing of someone who was totally unqualified for the job and someone I should have never inherited.

It was trial by fire. From the very first month, the administrative duties began to mount. The executive assessments and training Bob Slater had provided for me in Stuart a few years previous now came in handy. It was swim or drown. The months flew by and the church membership continued to keep pace with the rapid population growth. Soon I was responsible for providing music and personnel for seven services per week in four different musical styles. The forty-hour weeks of Alabama turned into eighty-hour weeks in Florida. Pastor was old-school and required six-day work weeks. Since I was

151

responsible for all seven services per week, I never got a full day off.

Fifteen years later during my first-ever Sabbatical in 2005, while reading my life journals chronologically, the stark realization dawned that those seven years at Church #4 were the only span of my adult life without a single entry. Not one. The pace and demands of the job were insane.

Not only did we do seven services weekly but the music team was also responsible for a Broadway-style Christmas musical, a dramatic Easter musical, a seven-day missions conference, a dramatic Fourth of July musical, and Pastor's pet project but my responsibility—the Country-Western Jamboree.

Not only did I face the challenge of producing and staffing all these events, but I was continually butting up against my old nemesis of legalism. My creativity kept me in hot water. And a conference our education pastor had us attend made matters even worse.

The seminar was held in Lakeland and the speakers were from a mega-church in Chicago that had gained international prominence with its unique "seeker-sensitive" methodology of ministry. Nancy Beach led the arts program there and presented a talk that grabbed my attention.

She advised us to form creative teams much like an advertising agency and she said artists were not called to be lone rangers. She suggested utilizing all forms of art in worship such as drama, dance, and poetry, as well as song. The ideas were new to me but they made sense. It was a captivating talk and it changed my ministry.

Pastor Bill Hybels talked about developing awareness of "seekers of God" in our services and admonished us to help them feel comfortable. He said that art and language convey volumes about who we are as a church. His talk made sense too.

Our pastor at Church #4 was all about evangelism and it was obvious that Hybels and his methodology was as well. It seemed a marriage made in heaven. But even though we discussed the contemporary methodology

152

afterwards on the ride home and in several staff meetings—I don't think he ever got it.

I immediately formed a creative team of artists (the other staff pastors soon jokingly called it my "dream team") and together we began to change the language of our services. The welcome and offering times were reconfigured to not embarrass new attendees and we added several forms of art, such as dramatic vignettes, short video clips from popular movies, and even began to occasionally add a "secular" song to the services—all themed with Pastor's message.

He agreed to prepare his messages a year in advance so the creative team had adequate time to prepare different genres of art around them and establish an overall theme for each service. Even though he had changed absolutely nothing about his preaching content and style—it had been the same way for twenty years and he believed the "if it ain't broke, don't fix it" philosophy—we were able to enhance his evangelistic style with the arts and this "seeker" methodology.

The jury was still out on what Pastor thought about it, but he put up with it because it was working. The church grew faster. And he loved my challenge for him to plan ahead.

It wasn't long, however, before this new way of doing church got me in trouble. I was summoned before the deacon board. The chairman was a redneck from Georgia. He was a big blustery man and one of those people who was always trying to be something he wasn't. He admonished everyone to save someone's soul and was a fanatic about an old-school program from Coral Ridge Presbyterian called *Evangelism Explosion*.

This story should be told for two pivotal reasons. The first was that during the entire meeting, Pastor did not say a word in defense of the new methodology. In fact, he didn't say a word at all. It took a while but it was starting to soak into this greenhorn that this "silence tactic" was a very good protection measure utilized by all pastors. It must have been taught in their seminaries.

153

Second was the reason for the meeting itself. The deacons (and especially the chairman) were upset that we had performed what they disdainfully called a "secular" song a few weeks ago during a church service. I realized this was a formal reprimand and furthermore, they asked me to cease and desist with any more of that "secular" music. They said the word *secular* like it was a filthy word.

I had already formed a theological opinion that there was no such thing as secular and sacred. It was either truth or it wasn't. And I felt that any art form was fair game as long as it measured up against what I coined the "truth" test. I had read the book *All Truth Is God's Truth* by Arthur Holmes and it made sense.

I had also tried to broach the subject and the book privately with Pastor but it was quickly obvious he just didn't get it. I believe the words were something like this: "Now Randy, I just don't know what to think about that…" And he then changed the subject.

It didn't take a rocket scientist to know that book with its "heathen" philosophy wasn't gonna fly with these religious Pharisees, so I decided to use a different approach. If you're gonna work at a mega-church, you better learn quick how to think on your feet.

I stood up during that meeting and said, "You know, that's too bad, because the Fourth of July musical is coming up and if I comply with your wishes, we will have to replace almost every song. That means we won't be able to sing songs anymore like 'The Star Spangled Banner' and 'When Johnny Comes Marching Home.' We won't even be able to do the song that recognizes all the Armed Forces with their secular theme songs."

Well, you should have seen those rednecks squirm. I had learned a long time ago if you want to put a few feathers in your cap, just do a rousing tribute to America and the Armed Forces. The Chairman blustered uncertainly, "Well, now, Randy, that's not what we're talking about here. Those songs aren't really secular. They're American."

154

I decided to try a little of that silent treatment the pastor was so good at. The meeting finally came to a clumsy end without a resolution. But, of course, I was urged to keep all those godly patriotic songs in the upcoming Fourth of July program, secular or not.

The battle with legalism continued. One Tuesday morning in staff meeting, another issue came to a head. This time with a clear and demonstrative end.

Staff meetings at Church #4 were corporate to a fault. They began with a devotion promptly at nine. It was unacceptable to be absent or late. A prayer time followed but was not to go past 9:45. Then the massive computer readout of the calendar was passed around and each event for the next week was meticulously read by Pastor's executive assistant.

The secretaries were dismissed at 10:15 and a report was given by each of the ten managers (i.e., kitchen, school, security, facilities, bookstore, etc.) followed by any necessary dialogue about calendar conflicts. The managers were dismissed at 10:45 and any assistant pastor who had an agenda item was allowed to speak. All agenda items for staff meeting were required to be presented in writing to Pastor's executive assistant by noon on Monday in order to be included. You were not allowed to speak to any item unless it had been approved and appeared on the agenda.

Finally at 11:30, the six of us who remained comprised the associate pastors and executive team. We were then allowed to address our agenda items. I started a tradition that all the pastors would go to a greasy-spoon Mexican place for lunch afterwards to build a sense of camaraderie. Our intense work schedules rarely bought us together and gatherings during the little free time we had after-hours were non-existent.

When all the pastors were gathered, there were over twenty in attendance at that third tier of the staff meeting at 10:45. It was at one of these times that the insidious hands (or should I say fist) of legalism withered away a little more of my soul.

One of the youth pastors was quite a jokester—in fact, he was an avid basketball player and was the one who had dubbed my group the "dream team" because of the amazing talent of the members. His wife (a creative genius and best-selling author) was on the creative team.

During the five-minute break after the managers were dismissed, we sat around the massive conference table and he began kidding me about the creative team's meeting on the previous Sunday evening. His wife had told him we were trying to figure out how to gently introduce dance during a service. The code word for the project was "planned movement." Southern Baptists have never been known for their love of dance—regardless of King David's example in the Old Testament—and we were trying to approach the powerful art form in a thoughtful and gradual way.

Somehow amid the din of conversation, Pastor heard the youth pastor's remarks. His fist slammed down on the conference table so hard our coffee cups rattled. A stunned silence filled the room. He stood up shaking in anger, looked me straight in the eye, and said, "Randy, as long as I'm pastor of this church, there will be *no* dancing! Period. End of discussion."

Nobody breathed. There was an uncomfortable but empathic embarrassment mixed with unspoken prayers of thanks that their names weren't Randy. After an uneasy few moments, the executive assistant timidly read the first item of the next agenda.

Afterwards the youth pastor apologized profusely to me for running his mouth and even Pastor found me and tried to explain his anger away as we walked into the restaurant for lunch. But the humiliation and damage was done. There was never a public apology for the way the matter was handled, and dance, the beautiful art form that was presented to God so often in scripture, was never permitted at that church.

The pastor wasn't the only one wound up tight. His wife was a bi-polar mixture of entitlement and paranoia. The ridicule and isolation by church members and area pastors' wives during the divorce and subsequent marriage had taken its toll. Being fourteen years younger than the pastor didn't help matters much either.

The Christian community may not have embraced her, but at Church #4, she was the first lady. And make no mistake, mega-churches are not democratic, nor theocratic; they are autocratic and she ruled her kingdom well. As in any major corporation, it's usually the person who sleeps with the CEO that really runs the company.

Autocracy and entitlement in a closed system like a mega-church works fine but when exposed to the real world, they just don't hold up as well. My oldest daughter and I got to see this play out in a hilarious way, and it had the added benefit of providing her an invaluable life lesson.

One of the perks of being a musician at a mega-church is the many travel opportunities that come your way. Pastor wanted me to lead music at the annual church ski trip in Montana. No one had to twist my arm and soon we were landing for a layover in snowy Minneapolis on the way to Bozeman. My girls had lived in the Deep South all of their lives and had never seen snow. Excitement was at a fever pitch.

This was in 1994, shortly before affordable cell phones appeared. As we deplaned an announcement came that our next flight (the last of the evening) had been canceled.

One of the newsletters my mentor Bob Slater had told me about was called *Bottom Line*. I recalled reading that when a flight is canceled the natural tendency is to rush to be first in line at the airline counter to reschedule. The handy little newsletter suggested rushing instead to the closest pay phone, calling the 800 number for the airline, and rescheduling with an operator. That way you could beat the long lines.

I was the only one who tried this new tactic, while the girls rushed with the others to grab a place in line, just in case. It worked. I managed to snag the last four tickets for the first flight to Bozeman the next morning.

As I smugly sauntered to one of the endless lines that wrapped around the airport lobby, I thought it best not to say anything. After suggesting my wife take our very tired and cranky eight-year-old daughter to a nearby seat, my oldest daughter who was a very cute eleven years old joined me waiting in line to get our paper tickets.

157

To her, it was a great adventure. There was snow outside the windows and I playfully placed my new Stetson cowboy hat (the church had purchased it for my first time as emcee of the Country-Western Jamboree) on her little head.

It just so happened that Pastor and his wife and their three children were directly in front of us in line. I realized immediately that the pastor's wife (who I barely knew) did not share our playful mood. She was not a happy camper. Her schedule had been screwed up and evidently that was not permitted.

Two-and-a-half hours later, around 1 a.m. in the morning, we finally reached a counter. I observed as my daughter watched—her big brown eyes growing in proportion to the pastor's wife's anger. As she berated the hapless ticket agent with Pastor looking on helplessly, I bent down and whispered to my daughter, "I think it might work better if both of us give the nice ticket agent a big smile instead of getting upset." She nodded and that big cowboy hat plopped cutely over her face.

We did indeed give that ticket agent her first smile in many hours and she returned the favor in spades. Before we left we had two complimentary adjoining deluxe rooms in Minneapolis' finest hotel, four breakfast vouchers at their fabled restaurant, round-trip cab fare to and from the airport, and tickets to the amusement park at nearby Mall of America, just in case we had time before our flight. She also informed me that I did indeed miraculously manage to secure the last four tickets for the next flight late morning to Bozeman.

The rooms were magnificent and the girls thought they had died and gone to heaven. Soaking in the ornate spa pool early the next morning, we recounted the moral of the story. The girls have never forgotten that trip. After a sumptuous breakfast accompanied by the lovely music of a string quartet, we rode the roller coaster at Mall of America and then just before noon slipped well-rested into those lovely four airplane seats. We were playing in the snow three hours later.

We learned the next day that Pastor, his wife, and three children had been given one room in a ratty Days Inn far

158

away from the airport. It was a honeymoon suite no less, with one king-sized bed and no shower; there was only a round bathtub in the middle of the room.

The kids had to stand backwards and hold bathrobes up in a circle to provide privacy as they each took a bath. They received no cab fare, no meal vouchers, and they did not get to ride the roller coaster at the mall. They had to wait at the airport all day after little sleep and finally managed to catch the last flight out late that evening.

My oldest daughter listened wide-eyed as they recounted their harrowing story. She then glanced my way and smiled knowingly. We thought it best not to tell them about our adventure. Almost twenty years later, as a grown woman, her life has taken her to exotic ports of call around the world and she has become a savvy and considerate traveler.

In the real world, a lowly airline employee trumps an entitled mega-church pastor's wife any day of the week.

159

# CHAPTER 14

# CHURCH #4
# (THE LATER YEARS)

Kelly was a tall flaming redhead with the most beautiful legs I had ever seen. She played oboe in the orchestra and all the woodwinds sat in the front row. Evidently her tanned and very long legs were giving some repressed jackleg in the audience inordinate fantasies.

Ironically, the complainant was not asked to attend counseling; in the evangelical church, it is always the woman's fault when a man lusts, so, of course, I was assigned the dubious task of asking her to cover up.

161

She was an earthy newcomer to the church scene and had obviously always enjoyed and savored life. Kelly and her husband were both well over six feet tall and were some of the most fun loving people I had ever met. The last thing I wanted was to put a sour taste in their mouths about church.

When she came to my office for her appointment, she grabbed a seat, unfolded those rangy culprits in front of me, and laughingly exclaimed, "Oh no, what did I do?" I awkwardly started to explain and each time words failed me. She finally said, "Oh hell, Randy. For God's sake, just spit it out."

I explained the situation to her and asked if she would mind possibly wearing longer skirts. Her freckled face reddened with a hint of anger as she told me it was almost impossible for a girl over six feet with long legs like hers to find a skirt that would be long enough to honor my request. She said most of her skirts *were* long. In fact, hers were longer than any other lady's in the orchestra—it was just that her damn legs were so freakin' long.

She then looked me straight in the eye and said, "I don't know what this guy's problem is; I wear panties when I come to church. The pervert needs to get a life."

This panty thing (or lack thereof) was just one of many issues my college education failed to address.

Another issue in which I had received absolutely no formal training from my university or church was the proper role of a pastor in death and dying.

About four years into my tenure at Church #4, I received a call that one of our choir members was dying. Jim was a gentle and kind soul who was a baker by trade. He was the jokester of the bass section and was a natural comic. He had a bushy silver beard and a ready smile. He had been unexpectedly diagnosed with cancer just a few weeks previous. It seemed impossible that he was already at death's door.

I called for information and found that hospice had already transferred him from the hospital to home to spend his last days. His wife was a precious lady and when I rang to inquire about Jim, she asked if I would be willing to

162

visit. She told me Jim really thought the world of me and it might do him some good. I agreed.

Upon arrival, I slipped back to their bedroom and gripped the cold steel rails of the hospital bed. The sterility of it stood in stark contrast to the rest of the cozy furnishings. The myriad IV lines hung limply as if they had sighed and given up. But the moment Jim saw me, his gray and sallow face lit up in a weak, warm smile. He tried to crack some sort of joke and then suddenly became serious.

He asked me to slide the rails down and sit on the bed, close by his side. Time melted away as we talked and a few hours later, he suddenly started shaking in terror, tears streaming down his face. He grabbed me in what seemed a death grip with his right hand and his wife with his left, and pulled us both very close to his warm face. His hot breath was like a perfume of cloying sweetness. He wept and sobbed, "I'm scared. I'm so scared. I don't want to die. Please don't let death take me away."

It was heartrending. The only thing I could think to do was softly sing one of the lullabies I had crooned to my girls long ago when they were fitful and couldn't sleep. Brahms always seemed to calm them somehow. As I tearfully sang, my voice breaking, then starting again, he calmed a bit. For the next few hours, Jim vacillated between agitated terror and eerie calm. I held him securely in my arms to calm his shaking and softly continued singing and humming.

Still struggling, he died in my arms as I was singing the old hymn "My Jesus I Love Thee." His wide-open eyes in death were still filled with terror. Jim was the first human being I had ever watched die slowly. The others had been sudden. All the touchy-feely stories I had heard from the pulpit about people sweetly calling out to angels as they died echoed eerily through my mind like hollow lies.

Jim had been one of the finest and most gentle men I had ever known. It took weeks for me to recover. It was as if the death angel decided to snatch away another part of my soul as he was rudely taking Jim. I had walked with Jim through the valley of the shadow of death and we had been afraid. There had been no rod and staff to comfort us.

163

Just as I was reeling from this confusing and devastating experience, I received an emergency page while serving my time as "Pastor on-call." Every ten weeks, everyone but the senior pastor was required to be on twenty-four-hour emergency call for a week.

Again there had been no training to help us triage the myriad crises. Our pastor often said that over twenty thousand people called our church their home. Those numbers always made it a tumultuous seven days and nights. The calls ranged from suicide attempts, child abuse, domestic disputes, emergency room visits, drownings, drug overdoses, car accidents, and deaths, just to name a few.

This particular call instructed me to rush to a local emergency room for an accidental death—the same mentioned earlier in chapter 11. When on-call week began, we were also issued one of the new mobile phones that were the rage. Driving frantically to the hospital, my phone started ringing. I slowly learned bits and pieces of the story. It seemed a fifteen year-old-member of our youth group had been struck by a car and killed during a church outing.

A church of our size was always a target for lawsuits, especially in the litigious climate of Florida, and even though we had received no pastoral care training, we had been required to attend lots of seminars about legal ramifications, liability, and malpractice. The hospitals were familiar with our church and always treated all the pastors like professionals. I was immediately escorted to the emergency room and then into the operating room.

Alayna's bruised and battered face lay in stark contrast to the swaddling bandages and white sheets. She was wrapped to her neck to protect the parents from any more shock than could be helped when they arrived. A trauma nurse stood stoically beside me in the cold still room and my eyes wandered aimlessly about—taking in the surreal scene—the lifeless body on the steel table surrounded by medical paraphernalia, which had been hastily moved to the perimeter of the room. The pungent smell of antiseptic burned my nostrils.

My phone buzzed and I was informed Pastor himself was on the way. There was fear of a lawsuit (and rightly so

—the family did indeed eventually initiate a massive lawsuit against the church *and* the youth pastor) and the voice on the line hinted that his calming presence might help matters. I was to stay and greet the parents if he did not make it before they arrived.

I will leave to your imagining the grim scene that followed.

Afterwards, just before sunrise, I trudged out to my car like a weary man old before his time and tearfully made my way home. I immediately slipped into each of my daughter's rooms and held them while sobbing an empty prayer of thanks they were still alive.

Numbness crept in. I didn't realize it then but my soul was slowly dying with each new tragedy. The insidious hands of the death angel had taken Mr. Brown, my voice teacher; Mr. Rosser in Alabama; Jim; and Alayna before my eyes. And now it was groping into the darkness of my soul. The visceral empathy with which I had been blessed was a curse again that night. As each person died, it was like a part of me died with them.

While it took me weeks to recover emotionally, it seemed as if Pastor was fine the next day. I couldn't understand how tragedies like this were just another normal day on the job for him.

I realize now that Pastor was a cognitive empath—gifted much like a therapist who can shut the door to the office after hours of hearing everyone's crap and leave it all behind. Humanity needs cognitive empaths to function as our psychiatrists, triage nurses, and emergency room physicians. The world would be in trouble without their gifts.

Pastors and volunteers who are cognitive empaths should be the staff members assigned to hospital visitation and on-call emergencies. Sending compassionate empaths such as myself into those situations is like injecting a slow-acting but deadly virus into their souls.

As religious leaders learn more about working in our strengths, I hope one day the Church will realize she is slowly but surely killing her creatives by requiring them to work in their weaknesses.

165

I pleaded to be released from hospital visitation and on-call responsibilities, but I was made to feel I was shirking my duty. And besides, I was told, in a corporate environment one must never set a precedent—what is required of one must be required of all.

Thankfully, even amidst all the death and dying, there was occasionally time to live a little.

Pastor was always planning destination revivals around wild adventure and hunting expeditions. One day at staff lunch while munching a burrito, Pastor asked out of the blue if anyone was afraid of grizzly bears. Eager to impress him (he rarely attended these lunches with his pastors), I reverted back to my Southern accent and casually drawled that I was not "afeared of no grizzly."

I should have had my head examined. In fact, I did a few years later. In 2012, my therapist gently educated me about the myriad complexities and problems of placing one's senior pastor in a father-figure role. My desire to please and exalt these men—who were human beings like me—increasingly caused me disappointment.

The next thing you know, an Alaskan bush plane was dropping Pastor and I hundreds of miles into the untamed wilderness of Kodiak Island with just a tent and a raft. As we gently slid to a perfect landing on the upper Uganik River, the pilot instructed us in a very serious and intense manner to be at the sandy beach on the right at the end of the river where the Gulf of Alaska begins five days hence. Or else.

As the plane took off, I experienced a feeling like none I had ever known. For the first time in my life, I felt the hair on the back of my neck stand up. I instinctively knew that I was now the prey and the grizzlies were the predator. I fervently wished that for once, I had listened to my reason instead of my consciousness.

Kodiak bears are a unique subspecies of the brown or grizzly bear. They live exclusively on the islands in the Kodiak Archipelago and have been isolated from other bears for about 12,000 years. There are about 3,500 Kodiak bears; a density of about 0.7 bears per square mile. But the density is even more pronounced in the Uganik River region.

166

You should also know that Kodiak bears are the largest bears in the world. A large male can stand over ten feet tall when on his hind legs, and five feet tall when on all four legs. They weigh up to 1,500 pounds. We encountered over forty bears during those harrowing five days with one coming into our campsite and brushing against our tent one night around midnight.

You really haven't lived until you need to go pee in the middle of the night, zip open the tent, and see a nine-foot, 1,200-pound brown bear just a few yards away silhouetted against an Alaskan moon, steam rising from his massive frame, while crunching the flesh and bones of an enormous silver salmon. I decided it best not to risk him thinking I was trying to mark my territory.

It *was* a fishing experience like no other and the fresh-caught salmon we cooked around the fire would melt in your mouth. Bald eagles soared above the waterfalls and we never saw the blight of another human being. It was an idyllic Garden of Eden—except for the bears.

They were everywhere. It was the only time in my life that I did not sleep for four nights straight. To put this experience in perspective, we were in the same region where the documentary *Grizzly Man* was filmed. And obviously we fared better than he or this book would not be in your hands.

One would think that a foxhole experience like this would bond the two of us as blood brothers forever. But Pastor had a unique way of compartmentalizing business and pleasure. Once back at the office in Florida, it was like the trip had never happened. It was business as usual.

Two events happened at Church #4 that eventually freed me from the mega-church pulpit and changed my life forever.

Because our church had over two thousand people in Sunday School (Bible study) attendance, I received an invitation to the *Metro Music Conference*. It was an exclusive club. Only fifty (male) pastors were invited from the largest Southern Baptist Churches in America. It was five days each year of music, teaching, and the latest mega-church gossip. The limited spots were highly sought after because the largest mega-church pastors would use the

167

*Metro Music Conference* directory to look for new hires for their vacant Minister of Music positions.

The first three years of attending the conference were really great. As a rookie, I was introduced to the latest television broadcast technology, met all sorts of interesting peers, and learned which mega-church pastors to never work with. It all seemed very novel. The locations and host hotels were always stunning and it was a gathering of extraordinary leaders and creatives.

However, it soon became obvious the old-school leaders of the group were still the alpha dogs creating the agenda. Even the younger guys who were slowly gaining power in the group were still working for ultra-conservative pastors.

Because of my new friendship with Nancy Beach, who had spoken at the conference I attended earlier, and the growing influence of Willow Creek Community Church, my personal philosophy of ministry was in the middle of a cataclysmic change. I felt increasingly out of place at the *Metro Conference.*

I wasn't learning anything new and the cost of the conference consumed all my budget allocation, so I skipped a year.

The following year I received a call from a long-time friend who was hosting *Metro* at his mega-church in Dallas. He said a lot of change had taken place and asked if I would be willing to speak at the conference.

He assured me I would be warmly received and told me he had also asked Rick Muchow, the music director of the innovative and fast-growing Saddleback Community Church in California, to join me as co-presenter.

Our presentation—a new way of doing church—was a rousing success. It seemed many of the old-guard Southern Baptist pastors were retiring, which was forcing many of the *Metro Music* guys to innovate—whether they wanted to or not. They were terrified of losing their jobs.

I enjoyed spending time with Muchow and several other new guys who were also at innovative churches, and the week was surprisingly pleasant. Many of them urged me to return for the next *Metro Conference* to be held in New York City. The host was to be Gary Moore and knowing the love for Broadway theatre that we both shared made it impossible to miss.

The story demands I go back in time for a moment. Gary was music director at the prestigious Second Baptist Houston and had previously served at the iconic First Baptist Church of Dallas. During my tenure at Church #1, our staff had traveled to First Dallas for their annual church conference called *School of the Prophets*. It was an old-school ultra-conservative harbinger to the Willow Creek and Purpose-Driven Conferences of today.

School of the Prophets was the brainchild of pastor W.A. Criswell, a revered leader of right-wing Baptists. The purpose of the conference was two-fold: to teach churches the First Baptist Dallas way of doing ministry; and second, to build alliances for the conservative battle against the moderates of the denomination.

Before we arrived in Dallas, I had called music director Gary Moore and scheduled an appointment to ask questions about music ministry. At that time, FBC Dallas was the largest and most wealthy church in America. I can only imagine what Gary thought when this redneck from a tiny country church in the Appalachians strolled into his office with a legal notepad and over fifty questions about choirs, microphones, growing a volunteer base, and selecting leaders.

Still, he treated me like royalty. I never felt rushed and Gary thoughtfully answered all my questions. I learned as much in that one hour as I did in some of my college classes. As I was leaving, he invited me to sing in the famous FBC choir that evening for the opening session of *School of the Prophets*.

It is hard to describe the awe I felt donning that choir robe and singing at the top of my lungs with seventy other members of the bass section in that four-hundred-voice choir. It was a pivotal moment of inspiration in my life. I knew then I was destined to lead a choir like this one day.

To make matters even more surreal, the choir member next to me was the bass section leader and obviously felt compelled to give this country hick an education. He was infinitely proud of his knowledge about the storied history of First Baptist Church, the choir, and Southern Baptists in

169

general. It was almost over the top to hear him go on, but I just politely smiled, nodded, and listened in awestruck wonder.

His chest puffed a bit as he told me that the speaker for the evening approaching the stage was Dr. Bailey Smith, the president of all (chest puffing a bit more) fourteen million members of the Southern Baptist convention, and a close friend of their pastor, Dr. Criswell. I replied like a humble redneck should with a reverent "you don't say."

Perhaps you can imagine the look on that Baptist boy's face a few moments later when Bailey (who just a few months previous had given me the "get yourself back to college talk") spotted me, excused himself from the plethora of dignitaries, and gave me a bear hug in front of the thousands of people assembled, saying, "Randy, what on earth are you doing here in this choir? It's so good to see you. Have you decided to attend college in Dallas?"

Out of the corner of my eye, I could see my self-appointed guide wilt like a week-old yellow rose of Texas as Bailey and I carried on like old pals. Yes, indeed, it was a grand moment.

Back to the present and Church #4. You now see why it was a special moment over twenty years later for Gary to personally call and ask *me* a favor. As host of *Metro Conference*, he was allowed to choose two registrants from a different denomination. He asked if I would invite my friends from Willow Creek Community Church in Chicago to attend. "Of course," I replied, "I would be thrilled to do so."

Maybe, just maybe, I thought, Baptists were finally moving into the twenty-first century. I promptly called and invited my friends who directed and coordinated the incredible worship teams at Willow. They agreed to attend.

The second day at *Metro Conference* in New York was a day that for me will forever live in infamy. As Scott and Vonda from Willow Creek sat beside me, a surprise speaker strolled unannounced into the room with his entourage. He was good friends and a business partner with the guy whose music company paid the expenses for most of the conference.

He was also the pastor of a church in Brooklyn that was famous for its choir, and along with several other well-known pastors at the time, was an outspoken critic of Willow Creek Community Church and its methodology. The room started to swim a bit as I feared the worst. I don't think he knew there were representatives from Willow Creek in attendance—but I doubt if it would have mattered.

He started with a vengeance. At first, he lashed out at our elite and wealthy *Metro* churches who knew nothing of what it was like to do ministry in a poverty-stricken urban environment like Brooklyn. Gathering steam, he preached against using anything other than a choir in worship, and then proceeded to his favorite subject of disdain, blasting Willow Creek and their "seeker-sensitive" heresy.

I was mortified. Afterwards, Scott and Vonda (always classy) tried to gently approach the pastor and ask if he had ever visited their church in Chicago to see for himself what it was really like. He reddened and stammered a defensive, "No, why would I need to *go* there?" And before they could say anything else, his entourage swept him away. Because he was not part of the conference, I had no further opportunity to speak with him.

That night I couldn't sleep. Finally, around 3 a.m. I got up and wrote a personal letter to that pastor from Brooklyn expressing my disappointment and embarrassment. I closed it with the lyrics to a song that longed for Christians to work together, not *against* each other.

The battle started. My reason screamed not to send it (Randy, just think of your career), but my consciousness could not abide what had happened that day. It just wasn't right.

I had spent my entire conference budget on this week in New York after working seven days a week for six straight years at Church #4. My fellow choir member Jim had died in my arms. I had to tell Alayna's parents she was dead. I was totally exhausted and in need of refreshment and encouragement, only to be harangued by an ignorant and insecure pastor who was threatened by the evangelism techniques of another much more famous peer.

I had my assistant mail the letter to him first thing the next morning and I asked Scott and Vonda to skip the

171

opening session the next day to spare them further embarrassment. As it convened, I read the letter to my *Metro Conference* peers. Instead of understanding and being open to dialogue, many of them ridiculed me. The others remained silent. I never went to *Metro* again.

I've often said that opportunity lies at the intersection of passion and need. That fateful day convinced me there was a need for a gathering of early adopting creatives and worship leaders that offered encouragement and refreshment.

My entrepreneurial fever rose. It was not from a desire to compete with *Metro*. At that time, in 1998, there were no worship conferences that focused on *being* rather than doing and that welcomed everyone, regardless of denomination and gender. Another huge value was to always include extended and open dialogue between the speaker and attendees.

A new conference was born. It first convened as *Beyond 2K* in 1999. Now called the *re:create Conference*, it gathers in Nashville, Tennessee, to this day.

A second entrepreneurial opportunity availed itself around this same time. Since the first Apple computer entered my life in 1984, I had been an early adopter for technology. The late 1990s was still a world without global search engines and I had been studying the philosophy of tech guru Tim O'Reilly and the always-controversial Steve Jobs.

I met with Pastor and told him about my idea for a new software program and that I planned to work on the project exclusively on my own time. I wanted to make sure the church would claim no intellectual privilege on an idea that was completely mine. He agreed and we shook on it. Every night for the next year, I worked on a new software that functioned like a search engine (this was just before the launch of Google) to aggregate all genres of creative arts.

When it was finally ready, I borrowed a shrink wrap machine, printed out crude labels, purchased shirt boxes in bulk for packaging, and copied the floppy discs by hand—one at a time.

The software package debuted at the *InfoComm Conference* in Dallas. I took twenty-five packages and priced them at $150 each. They sold out in fifteen minutes before the conference even started. It was obvious I had something big. I had just made a month's salary in fifteen minutes.

I would barter exhibit booth space at conferences in return for presenting a talk called "Worship on the Bleeding Edge." Without realizing it, the talk perfectly set up a demand for my software. It was called Creative Assistant and it sold out at every conference that year. It wasn't long before there were offers to buy my idea. By this time, it was autumn of 1999, the Nasdaq was hitting record highs every day and tech was the buzzword on Wall Street.

The insane work schedule at Church #4 combined with the rollout of the software took a huge strain on me physically. At the cusp of a new millennium, days before the New Year of 2000, I was bedridden with a severe case of pneumonia.

Still in the middle of my illness, the phone rang and Pastor (who never called) was on the other end of the line. He asked me to come into the office for a meeting that afternoon. It didn't seem to matter to him that I had pneumonia. A sense of foreboding permeated my being.

I knew there was trouble the moment I walked into Pastor's office, still foggy from medication. The new executive pastor who had recently been hired from the business world somberly stood as I entered. It was one of those times when everything seems to be floating around with a disembodied surrealism.

Pastor was not one for small talk and jumped right in saying, "Randy, we've gone too far with this contemporary worship stuff. We need to set the ship aright." Through my drug-induced fog, I struggled to understand what he was saying. I asked, "Are you firing me?"

In his thick south Arkansas accent he replied, "No, no, noooo, Randy, I'm not firing you. It's just that the worship pendulum (he gestured to his left like the hands of a clock) was over here around 4 p.m. when you came; we've now swung over to about 8 p.m. (he gestured to the right.) I'm just asking you to move it back to the middle (he moved both hands to the middle) somewhere around 6 p.m. or so."

I hoarsely asked, "If you're not firing me, why is the executive pastor here? We've always talked about issues just the two of us. I don't understand." I continued, "And Pastor, you know I'm asked to speak all over the country about contemporary worship. You know I believe with all my heart that this new way of doing church is what will propel us into the next millennium. I don't think I can do what you are asking long-term. But as long as I'm here, you know I will honor your wishes."

He blustered, "No, no, no, I'm not firing you and I don't want you to think about long-term anywhere but here. We just need to swing the pendulum back to the middle, that's all." Of course, there was the obligatory closing prayer to make everything okay and I walked out of his office knowing my days at Church #4 were numbered.

My life-long nemesis—depression—set in with a vengeance. I didn't get out of bed for five days straight. But the show must go on, sick or not.

As we joined each other on stage the next weekend for services, Pastor could see the hurt in my eyes. While the multitude of thousands flocked in, he whispered, "I can see I've hurt you; that was not my intention." I replied, "That's okay. I just don't know what to do."

It was time to begin, so I flashed a big smile, hid my hurting heart, and stepped out front to lead the first of five capacity crowds that weekend in worship.

Another one of those fateful calls came a few days later from a mega-church just outside of Nashville, Tennessee. Their former music director (a *Metro Music Conference* member) had resigned his position after twelve years because the church wanted to institute more contemporary services. He told them if they truly wanted someone who thrived on innovation—they should call me.

The offer they presented was too good to pass up. It would double my salary, provide a substantial signing bonus, and I could also bring along two long-time

174

members of my team and give them significant salary increases.

That "doubling salary thing" sounds really impressive until you understand the conservative salaries at Church #4. Two of the assistant pastors were so poorly paid, they qualified for government help and accepted food stamps to get by.

The clincher for this new church came when I found out how many services I would be responsible to lead each week. Instead of seven services a week, they had only two. They worked a five-day week (instead of the six-day week at Church #4) and if that weren't enough, after five years of service, I would receive a month-long sabbatical in addition to my vacation. There was also talk of a golf membership.

The depression miraculously lifted and as I contemplated a return to the hills of Tennessee, I started humming and singing the theme song of the Beverly Hillbillies television show. "You're all invited back again to this locality. To have a heapin' helpin' of their hospitality."

There were many positive learning experiences at Church #4. Pastor was very conservative financially and had challenged me to erase all my depreciating debt by age forty. I was able to accomplish that task. I had grown equity in a Florida home. I learned how to lead a team and received an education in church politics. I had also created two successful businesses.

The multi-ethnic one-hundred-plus voice choir had grown and flourished. We had recorded and produced a live worship album at the request of a famous Nashville music label. We began writing the script and music for our own Broadway-style Christmas musicals. And the church had grown steadily during those years.

But for some reason, Pastor never bought into a new way of doing church. He was set in his ways. His old-school methods had always worked and I guess he figured they always would. Even though he begrudgingly agreed in the later years to let me shed my coat and tie for our casual service, he just couldn't take his off. Some things were just not going to change.

So I loaded up the truck and moved to Tennessee.

175

# CHAPTER 15

# CHURCH #5
# (THE EARLY YEARS: THE COUNTRY CLUB)

Spring was lifting her skirts. The sweet bouquet of honeysuckle smelled like homemade Tennessee wine and looking at the vivid yellow of wild daffodils in verdant green fields gave me a wonderful sense of déjà vu. Even the dirt smelled fresh and familiar as I bent down to repair a golf divot.

The wining and dining during the interview process for Mega-church #5 had displayed Southern hospitality at its best. A luxurious Marriott in an affluent suburb of Nashville had replaced the fleabag hotel of Church #4. Beautiful gift baskets greeted my girls and me providing fresh flowers, Goo-Goo clusters, Sun-Kist Cola, and movie tickets for the opulent theatre next door.

177

It was already a done deal. I had accepted the lucrative offer and Pastor and I were celebrating with a round of golf at his private club. The course was immaculate. And ritzy. It was a place to see and be seen. The clubhouse dining room had been tapped by a local magazine as the most likely place to see a celebrity in Nashville.

But more importantly to me, I was back home in Tennessee. The exclusive country club with its laminated scorecard and plush leather seats was a far cry from the mountain store with its faded checker board and barrels on the porch in Beersheba. But when you got right down to it —it accomplished the same thing: good ole male bonding and testosterone-filled competition. Some things never change.

As we rounded hole number ten, Pastor told me he had been looking for a soul mate. Someone who shared his philosophy of ministry. He, too, had been influenced greatly by Willow Creek and he wanted to change the way Church #5 was doing ministry. He felt we could be a team made in heaven. It sounded too good to be true.

Pastor was a uniquely built man. Standing about five-foot-seven, he was quite a bit shorter than me. But he was big. Really big. Weighing almost three hundred pounds, he was one of those guys who always struggled with weight. He had rheumy eyes that were light bluish and thin blonde hair tinged with gray.

As we discussed the first Sunday I would be on stage, he said, "And, oh, Randy, I know you are accustomed to leading the worship music, and that is certainly what you will be doing. But your first Sunday you won't have to worry about leading; I just want you to sing a solo." I asked who would be handling the worship responsibilities and he casually replied, "Michael W. Smith."

"So let me get this straight, Pastor. Arguably the most famous male singer in all of Contemporary Christian music will be leading worship my first Sunday and you want *me* to sing a solo?" As we approached the tee at hole number 11, he looked at me with a challenge in his eye and a half-smile on his lips and said, "That's right. Can you handle it?" I gathered myself and replied, "Yes, of course, I can."

It was quickly dawning on me that even though I was back in Tennessee, Nashville was a much different world than the region a hundred miles southeast where I had grown up. In fact, I was soon to find out that Nashvegas (as it was affectionately called) was different than any place on earth.

Michael W. Smith did indeed lead worship in both services my first Sunday in April 2000. I managed a solo and afterwards we lunched in a private room at the country club. Smitty (as he is known to his friends) and his wife joined me and Pastor and our wives at a beautiful table overlooking the first fairway. As our children chatted at a separate table, we adults talked life in Nashville. It did not seem real.

It was late afternoon when we finished and I slipped into the men's locker room to splash water on my face. Pastor came in and stood beside me. "You all right?" he asked. I nodded and the next words he uttered could not have been more prophetic. "Be careful, Randy. Nashville will get into your head. Just be yourself. People here just need Randy to be Randy. Don't ever try to be something you're not and you will get along just fine."

Truer words could not have been spoken.

They say it differently in the mountains: "Everybody's mess stinks. If you try to act like yours don't, people won't be as apt to take a shine to you."

Three things caught me by surprise at Church #5. First, I was back in the Bible Belt. You don't realize what that's like until you've been away from it for almost two decades. Except for the three short years in south Alabama at Church #3, I had been blissfully away from the close-minded thinking of Southern evangelicals for most of my ministry.

Second, I didn't realize that Nashville was the Southern Baptist version of Mecca. The downtown cityscape was dominated by skyscrapers emblazoned with the *LifeWay* logo. Formerly known as the Southern Baptist Sunday School Board, *LifeWay* stockpiled millions of dollars by capitalizing on its fourteen million church members' weekly need for conservative Bible-based curriculum.

179

The long-term president and officers of *LifeWay* wielded the real power in the denomination. A different mega-church pastor was elected President of the Southern Baptist Convention every year but could only serve one additional term for a maximum of two years. It was largely a figurehead position.

Most of the old-school leaders of *LifeWay* (including the President) attended Church #5 when I came on the scene. Let's just say they were not fans of a new way of doing church.

Third was the presence of the contemporary Christian music industry. Nashville was home to the big three Christian record companies (all who by this time had been purchased by major labels) and so it was also the place where most of the recording artists lived. Most of them had been abruptly displaced and they had no church home or mentors in their lives.

Ever the idealist, to me these three diverse factors had the potential for an incredible renaissance. If ever there was a church that could influence the arts in a positive way, it was this one. Now more than ever, I felt I had been called to change the world.

My first Sunday leading worship was another instance of déjà vu. As I stood there in front of thousands of people, I realized I had previously lived this moment down to the last detail. The people, the church, the architecture, even the color of the carpet had been in a dream I had had over fifteen years earlier. It was eerie. Perhaps it was destiny.

However, there was a lot to do before we could get down to the business of changing the world. Church #5 had not made as much progress in their transition from traditional Southern Baptist church to contemporary church as they had led me to believe. I walked into a maelstrom.

As the motors for the enormous velvet stage curtain hummed softly and began to open, our extraordinary orchestra (better than most city symphonies) began to play a rousing tune and the signal came from the stage manager for me to walk out front and center and begin my first Sunday as worship leader.

It was like the *Tonight Show*. As I walked through the curtain, I felt like any moment someone like Ed McMahon would say, "Heeeeeeeeere's Randy!" The choir was replete in sequined gowns and the rhythm section could have been led by Doc Severinsen. This showboat opening was not me.

I was shocked. Worship with Michael W. Smith the week before and the videotapes Pastor had previously sent me to illustrate their worship style had been nothing like this. I soon found out this showy style was what a normal weekend at Church #5 was really like. Pastor had not yet communicated his new philosophy of ministry. As the days passed, it seemed he had not communicated much of anything.

Carrying a packing box to unload in "my office" the next morning, I encountered one of the other pastors who had been temporarily heading up the worship arts team sitting at my desk. It was immediately obvious he had not been told to vacate in preparation for my arrival. I apologized, backed out, and finally stacked my belongings in the workroom by the copier. The young lady sitting at the entry office whom I had been told would be my personal assistant realized something was amiss and followed me to the crowded back room.

As I reclined against the photocopier and she plopped on a work table, I started asking questions. Lots of them.

It quickly became apparent that *no one* on the worship arts team knew I had been hired to lead the team. It wasn't until several years later that I learned from the newly hired executive pastor—who was a long-time church member—I was the only executive staff member to be hired without a vote from the congregation in the 120-year history of the church. Not only did my team not know why I had been hired—neither did the church.

The honeymoon was over that first hour in the copy room. It was a dismal foreshadowing of the next six years. The contrast to my previous Church #4 could not have been more stark. There were no regular staff meetings, the doors to the multi-million dollar auditorium were never locked, the arts staff had no specific work hours or responsibilities, and nothing was in writing; the church was paying me a six-figure salary and no one even knew I was the Pastor of Arts.

It got worse. There had been no strategy put in place to effect change and the contemporary worship style that Pastor hired me to do created massive fallout. To make matters even more horrific, the unrest caused Pastor to handle those days like a bull in a china shop. The change was too fast and too abrupt. Good people were leaving in droves. A sermon (that was soon known as the "bus" sermon) caused even more people to depart.

In that talk, Pastor quoted Robert Schuller, a mega-church pastor in California, who had said, "Every chance at success is like riding the bus. If you are not prepared and courageous enough to get on the bus before it departs, you will miss your opportunity for success."

Many people thought Pastor was saying that if they were not prepared and courageous enough to get on the bus of the new worship style, they should get off. I don't think he meant that, but a lot of the old-school members sure did.

A traditional (and proud of it) Southern Baptist church in a neighboring suburb gained so many of our exiting members they had to build a new sanctuary; and over the next thirty-six months of our transition were voted one of the fastest growing churches in the nation. Most of the Baptist leaders from *LifeWay* also left and rumors swirled they were praying for our transition to fail.

Even the national Baptist newspaper blasted our "worship wars." It was a tough time for Pastor who had previously been the golden boy being groomed for president of our denomination. The Southern Baptist power brokers had used him—Pastor later told me the Seminary board meetings were endless and consumed his life for over two years—to install an ultra-conservative president in a nearby Baptist seminary. But even though they had used his power and influence to do their dirty work, when the transition started at our church they turned their backs on him.

During the next few years over one thousand people left. To make matters even worse, many of our best

182

financial contributors departed to the nearby church I previously mentioned.

Pastor went into clinical depression and was often absent from his leadership position in the office. Several times we were forced to show the second Sunday service a video of his message from the first service because he did not have the strength to preach twice.

It was in this climate of religious despair that I watched the first plane hit the World Trade Center on September 11, 2001. It seemed the whole world was going down in flames. Both the church and now our nation were disintegrating before my eyes.

I'm sure you can still remember what you were doing at that precise moment. I was at my favorite coffee shop in our historic suburban town at a mentoring meeting with musician Mark Lee. He is co-founder of the Christian rock group *Third Day* and had been attending our church. We became friends and also developed a mentor-protégé relationship. Neither of us will ever forget that fateful morning.

We immediately drove to the church conference room to watch the news on the television with members of the church staff. Calls began coming in from artists across the region asking what they could do and we soon started working on a memorial prayer service for that evening.

It was a somber gathering that night; the church was packed to overflowing. Michael W. Smith played the piano and sang melody and I sang harmony along with two other recording artists from our church, Rebecca St. James and Wendi Green. I can still hear Smitty leading out, "Above all powers, above all kings, above all nations and all created things, above all wisdom, and all the ways of man; You were here, before the world began."

That night I learned Pastor was at his best when tragedy strikes. He liked performing. He liked being onstage, being the center of attention, and doing something he did with supreme excellence. Like many preachers I know, he was not good at rejoicing and celebrating but he excelled at delivering heartfelt and tear-filled eulogies.

183

We needed to cry that night. It was a service I will never forget and I was proud to be a part of it.

In times of deep suffering, two things provide me solace: books and running. By this time I was training for my eighteenth marathon. I had started running long distance during my college years at Palm Beach Atlantic and it was one of the joys of my life. It was great discipline for my artistic bent and those peaceful hours of running (most of them alone) provided much-needed respite from the melee of the ministry.

Books also provided welcome relief. Tomes such as *Walking on Water* by Madeline L'Engle, *Beauty* by John O'Donohue, *Out of Solitude* by Henri Nouwen, and *Blue Arabesque* by Patricia Hampl provided a new (and sometimes taboo) way of thinking about the world.

I had been invited to attend a small group Bible study with Pastor and five other men. It was at the ungodly hour of 6:30 a.m. on Wednesdays, but each week I would somehow drag my night owl self out of bed to be there, desperate for any connection time I could have with the pastor. Early in my mega-church years, I found that everybody wanted time with the senior pastor but almost no one ever got it.

One morning as we discussed the topic of heaven, and remembering that Pastor had expressed interest in a soul mate relationship with me during the interview process, I decided to test the waters. Throwing caution to the wind, I said, "Sometimes when I'm lying on my pillow in the darkness of the night, I have times when I doubt if heaven is real. Do any of you guys ever feel that way, or am I the only one?"

The library where we met each week filled with a heavy quiet—a hidden silence. Memories of growing up flooded my reason as I recalled frequently making situations reticent and uncomfortable. I empathically sensed a disquiet.

The men in the room seemed afraid to say the wrong thing so no one said a word. After a long pause, Pastor said, "No, Randy, I can honestly say I've never felt that way." Another pregnant moment went by and Pastor shifted to the next subject without any further acknowledgement of the weight of that moment. I was crushed.

I had recently read that one of the ways to develop a deep friendship—an *Anam Cara* relationship—as O'Donohue calls it, " . . . is to listen compassionately and creatively to the hidden silences. Often secrets are not revealed in words, they lie concealed in the silence between the words or in the depth of what is unsayable between two people."[3]

The words that were *not* said to me during the vulnerability and honesty of that juncture spoke volumes. I longed for someone to hear me in the silence, to acknowledge the existence of doubt, and courageously attempt to dialog words that were thought unspeakable.

The sobering realization dawned that Pastor did not want a soul mate; he just wanted someone to fill his empty space so he did not have to face it. And now I was that someone. A few days later, another staff member bitterly confided in me that he had formerly been the "chosen one, the soul mate," but since I entered the scene, he had been abruptly forgotten.

The golf course was the place of escape for Pastor from the pain of transition at church, and as his appointed "soul mate," that evidently meant being there with him at all times. As his employee, I was required to be on-call, ready to accompany him to the links at a moment's notice. Sounds wonderful, doesn't it?

However, as my handicap (my average golf score) decreased, my empathic burden of Pastor and his angst increased. You can learn at lot about a guy on a golf course. During the interview process and when we golfed with others, he was the perfect gentleman and insisted on following the rules to the letter. When we were alone, all etiquette was out the window.

He would take a shot immediately when he got to his ball—even if by rule it was my turn; he would walk on my putting line on the green (a huge breach of etiquette), shove the flag in the hole before I putted out, and many

---

[3] John O'Donohue, *Anam Cara: A Book of Celtic Wisdom.*

times he would not take the time to record my score. My words would hang in the air without reply and eventually evaporate.

I realized I was nothing more than his employee. The only reason he wanted me on the golf course was to keep him company. He was priority number one, and there was no number two. He not only valued loyalty, he demanded it. The Faustian pact this entailed began putting a strain on my real life and my marriage.

Pastor, like many mega-church ministers, didn't like to go home. Domestic life bored him. His children challenged him with responsibilities that he didn't want. I often witnessed them, as young adults, belittle and ridicule him in front of others in public. He took it without saying a word in defense. In a strange way, I think it was his penance for being absent most of their lives.

Home might not have been a pleasant place, and he often avoided the office, but nowhere was Pastor more pampered, more doted upon, more satisfied, and freer to explore and indulge the far boundaries of his pastorness than on Sundays. The pulpit was his Shangri-la.

One week as our creative team fretted about the way to present a controversial idea, Pastor said, "It's not your job to worry about how I say things. I can spin anything. I don't care what it is." And spin he did. Never a victim of groupthink, he sincerely believed he was the Lord's anointed when in the pulpit, and many times his staff were the ones left to pick up the pieces and execute some wild and impromptu idea that came from his proverbial spinning.

He relished Sundays and the stage, but it was becoming increasingly clear he wanted all the authority but none of the responsibility during the week. And it was dawning on me that whenever something went wrong in his life, I was going to take some crap for it. I had failed to fulfill his longing for a soul mate.

We all want to believe in the existence of heroic figures —stronger and wiser than ourselves—to whom we can turn for an answer to all our vexation and grief.

I had developed expectations about how my leaders would treat me based on my relationship with my parents.

186

My parental relationships were, for the most part, emotionally nourishing and respectful of my rights and feelings (except for my hair); so I grew up expecting others to support me in much the same way.

The expectations I had for my senior pastors were unfairly based on a life-long quest for a wise guide with an internalized consciousness. A mentor who knew his real self. All my life, I had looked to others for answers that needed to come out of the depths of my own being.

During this tumultuous season of soul searching, occasionally there would be lighter moments. Pastor's addiction to golf provided several of those times.

One afternoon I received a summons to be in front of his office at 7 a.m. the next morning, golf clubs in hand. He also said we wouldn't be home until late that night. Like a good boy, I rang my personal assistant and asked her to cancel my appointments for the day.

It was a glorious early summer morning in Tennessee— not a cloud in the sky. Two other members of Pastor's entourage (guys in our 6:30 a.m. Bible study) were there before me, ready for a fun day on the links. We all loaded our clubs, grabbed steaming cups of coffee, and headed north on the interstate without a clue to our destination.

There was an easy and content quiet in the SUV. Pastor's retinue was accustomed to lengthy periods of silence when traveling with him. He was never at a loss for words when in the pulpit, but most other times he was not one to engage in useless conversation.

Heading east on I-40, we took the airport exit. Our curiosity was piqued by the suspense. We parked at the executive section of the airport and received orders to unload our bags. A few minutes later, we were boarding a small gulfstream jet, the three in the entourage looking at each other, raising our eyebrows in surprise and excitement. This was shaping up to be a good day.

As we settled into the plush leather couches on each side of the well-appointed plane, none other than former Lt. Col. Marine (now *Fox News* celebrity) Oliver North sat before us. He had obviously spent extended time in air travel. His salt-and-pepper hair was perfectly coifed and his legs were crossed in the casual manner of his

187

demeanor; the expensive cloth of his elegant wool slacks hung perfectly, every crease in place, and black wingtips perfectly shined.

He was shuffling a sheaf of notes in his lap but had a ready smile and greeting for us. Despite his pleasant and charismatic countenance, his eyes looked tired.

Colonel North (dare I call him Ollie?) told us he had an all-day speaking gig in Nashville and that his jet—which would just be sitting here all day—was at our disposal for a nice destination golf outing. He asked Pastor, "Which way will you be heading? North, South, East, or West?"

Sinking deeper into the soft Corinthian leather—as if in some sort of crazy dream—as the uniformed co-pilot asked what we would like to drink, for some reason, my first thoughts were of how I was going to explain this to my mom and dad. I was not a *Fox News* fan (nor any other news channel, for that matter), but my parents were addicted. To this day, I think they believe that Fox News and the Holy Bible are equally inspired, inerrant, and breathed by God.

I never found out why we had opportunity to avail ourselves of Mr. North's jet that day and I didn't ask. Unlike my parents, I know way too much about the inner workings and power brokering of conservative politics and mega-church religion.

Let's just say the same redneck kid who followed orders and stoked the old coal stove in a tiny three-room house that was falling down in the middle of Appalachia was the same kid (just thirty years older) who followed orders and flew on Lt. Col. Oliver North's gulfstream jet to the coast of Florida. That kid played golf (very well that day, I might add) at one of the finest courses in the world, had a sumptuous meal complete with linen and silver, enjoyed a glass of the finest wine on the way back home, and slept in my own bed that night.

The next day that redneck kid, now back to the real-world of being a renaissance man, got up to the pulpit once again to sing a lullaby (of sorts) for a hurting and bleeding mega-church. But hope was in the air. Over the next three years, the church began to slowly recover and grow.

But as the church experienced a rebirth, my soul continued to wither away. Just as Pastor had longed for me to be his soul mate, I was desperate for one of my own.

# CHAPTER 16

# CHURCH #5
# (THE LATER YEARS)

Colorful multi-story buildings filled with expensive antiques line the idyllic Main Street of the historic suburban town where Church #5 is located. The overpriced furniture perfectly fits a lifestyle that makes no apologies for being luxurious, and the metaphor for that world is the houses that people live in, which are much too big for their lives. You can find 80,000-square-foot homes inhabited by a husband, wife, and one child, and there is something both seductive and obscene about that lifestyle.

I was descending a very narrow and perfectly creaky staircase in one of those establishments when a tall blonde guy and his attractive wife backed down the landing to let me descend. As I squeezed past with eyes down to make sure my size-twelve feet didn't miss a step, he drawled, "How you doing, Randy?"

191

I was accustomed to being recognized and replied, "Fine, thanks, please excuse me," and politely slipped by. Not until I safely reached the bottom step did it register that the couple who had greeted me by name was Alan and Denise Jackson.

The superstar singer and his wife had been attending our church for the past few months, but it was still hard to recognize him without his ever-present cowboy hat. He had just released an album of old hymns called *Precious Memories*, and it was selling like hotcakes. In an interview with *Billboard Magazine* the week before it published, he had mentioned our church and said that the music he enjoyed there was quite different from this album.

It may seem odd that I would not have recognized a celebrity of his caliber until you realize the thousands of people who attended our church each Sunday meant that I was frequently approached in public—and always watched.

One evening at a posh restaurant, while in the middle of a dinner date with my wife, a couple interrupted us saying they attended our church and it made them feel so good to see their pastor say grace before a meal. As soon as they were out of earshot, I started griping. "Can you imagine the nerve of that couple to think that praying over our dinner makes us any more holy?" I seethed.

Previously at Church #4, I would grab a pizza and blanket and take the girls to the beach each Friday for sunset. Inevitably our rare and precious family time would be rudely interrupted. It would infuriate me that people were so thoughtless.

And while my notability was nothing compared to a celebrity like Alan, there is a fair amount of discomfort that comes from the feeling of never being alone. As a kid, I bitterly disliked people coming to our parsonage unannounced when we lived on the mountain.

Even though people think I am an extrovert due to my stage persona—in reality, I am an introvert. All the personality assessments I've taken prove this out. I like my privacy and unfortunately for most of my life, it has been virtually non-existent.

An increasing number of celebrities were attending our church and as I got to know them, I empathized with the lack of alone time in their lives. Solitude brought restoration to my being, but there was very little to be had.

I also empathized with the weariness I had seen that day in Oliver North's eyes. I was tired. A weariness was slowly seeping into my soul like a chilling anesthetic.

My cell phone rang a few days after seeing Alan, and a terse voice instructed me to get to the local hospital immediately. The chairman of the deacons at our church had suffered a heart attack. I was the staff member who lived closest to the hospital and as fate would have it, I arrived before anyone else. Again I was escorted into a sterile room filled with bright lights surrounding a stainless steel operating table. The air was so cold I looked for fog on my breath.

The once-vibrant man now lying rigid on the table, paleness taking color from his flesh, had not been a fan of this new style of worship. He had let Pastor know that fact in no uncertain terms. But he had been a good man. And a good man is hard to find.

Always wise and kind, he had provided solid leadership during our difficult transition as a church. But the worries of a business, combined with growing concern for his church had been more than his mortal body could take.

Sobs racked my body in empathic compassion. The death angel, my dubious companion, sucked a little more life out of my soul for good measure.

Pastor arrived a few moments later and the honest violence of his emotion made me cringe. He prostrated himself over his deacon's body and moaned a faint cry that was profound in its grief. He did not want to face up to this death. Yet he instinctively knew that, during this moment, unless he managed some sense of closure, he might have to suffer it for the rest of his life. He somehow composed himself just as the family entered the death-filled room with their own wails of disbelief and shock.

In the days that followed, those who knew me best knew something was not quite right. But no one paused to consider why.

My wife stumbled onto a sketch I had done during a recent solo escape to the beach and gave me an easel for Christmas. She was busy and thriving at a new career in real estate and felt I needed a hobby. She said, "You are a work-a-holic and this might provide a relaxing outlet on your off days."

I decided to give it a try. I had read somewhere the foundation for a strong watercolor was a good sketch. Graphite drawings were a particular love of mine, so I purchased an inexpensive set of pencils, watercolors, brushes, a John Pike palette, and a couple of sheets of handmade watercolor paper.

The way I learn best is by reading. So I found a few books on watercolor and consumed them. One statement in particular hooked me into this medium: "There are no mistakes in watercolor. Let the liquid flow, a life of its own, into magic spaces and then become one with the art. Forget time as we know it. Watercolor is art. And time does not exist in art."

A lifetime photography buff, by combining my digital camera and watercolor, I discovered a nuanced appreciation for the play of light on surfaces, of shadows in nature, and later on the beauty of the human form. I eagerly devoured Irving Stone's fascinating books about Pissarro, Van Gogh, and Michelangelo. I looked forward to Saturdays, my day set aside to paint, with eager anticipation.

I would start painting in the early morning and ten hours would go by as if they were seconds. For the first time in my life, I truly understood the famous phrase from the movie *Chariots of Fire,* "When I run, I feel God's pleasure." When I painted with watercolors—more than leading worship for thousands, more than any previous life activity—I felt God's pleasure.

This art form provided another benefit as well. It was cathartic. My real self had never been able to escape totally from its religious prison. Painting broke loose creative aspects of my being; but unfortunately the rest of my capacities remained caught in developmental arrest.

I learned anew that my birthright was creativity. The ability to invent, to perceive old patterns in new relationships, and to arrange old patterns in new ways, created a growing hunger for self-expression and enabled me to express my inner feelings.

194

But this new method of expression created a conflict unlike anything I had ever experienced—a struggle with my own personal muse. Watercolor was becoming the primary path in an existential quest for my real self. I was discovering freedom—but it was like forbidden nectar.

The Appalachian Mountains that were my native home served as a fitting metaphor for the defenses I had erected around my imprisoned self. Before now, only my singing and the acknowledgement and approval of my talent freed the creative capacity of my real self from that psychic prison. But my painting was activating and consolidating the creative (and withered) aspects of my soul. As I tapped into this new reservoir of creativity, I fulfilled the expression of my true self.

But the other six days when I returned to the real world of the ministry, my self was to be denied. To reiterate: Pastor was priority one and there was no number two.

Our church was coming out of the transition. It was a rebirth of monumental proportions. Before the upheaval, the average age of a church member was in the mid-forties. Now the average age was twenty-eight. We had recovered the lost numbers and had grown even larger than before. Several successful young businessmen had more than made up for the lost contributions.

We had two rock-star youth pastors and on Sunday we had hundreds of teenagers providing an energy to our worship services like few of us had ever witnessed. Every Sunday was electric. The musician pool in Nashville is world-class and each week I was surrounded by Grammy-winning instrumentalists and the finest studio vocalists. It was a musician's dream come true. For me, leading worship in this environment was simple—get it started and get out of the way.

By this time, the choir and orchestra were things of the past. Their demise had come at great cost, but to Pastor they had been a means to an end. But things change fast and even the Willow Creek–style of highly programmed worship was becoming old-school.

The new style of worship that was the rage at this time was a rock-like band and a lead singer with a couple of people singing loose harmony. An English worship

195

movement featuring the likes of Matt Redman and a band called *Delirious* had revolutionized contemporary Christian music and thus the church. Or was it the other way around?

I'm not sure, but this organic worship movement spawned all sorts of creative energy. The band that led worship during our youth services was called *Paramore* and before long became an award-winning multi-platinum pop punk band touring the world.

Our church was hosting the nation-wide conferences for a new movement called *Worship Together* and our stage was frequently filled with the creatives and artists who were changing the religious world.

Celebrities like Billy Ray Cyrus and his family, including thirteen-year-old daughter Miley who had just snagged a role in the movie *Big Fish*; Faith Hill, Lee Greenwood, Daniel Bedingfield, Dave Mustaine of Megadeath, and many others were sporadically showing up at our church. The energy of our services was also attracting most of the up-and-coming Contemporary Christian music groups.

Pastor moved slow (he still had the Willow Creek needle) and this new style of worship, which embraced moments of silence between songs and demanded less seamless production and more spontaneity, was way outside his comfort zone. As the creative team tried to adjust to the organic changes in our church, he became increasingly discomfited.

The nasty remark, the stony silence, the surprising indifference—they had been part of his repertoire ever since the honeymoon was over, but they were usually sporadic interruptions to a generally more genial mood. Now these stormy moments came more frequently, and there was an overall harshness, an impatient intolerance that wasn't there before.

I don't know what they teach mega-church pastors in seminary, but for some reason they feel they must become superhuman. And indeed they are for a while. The psychosis of religious people demand it. But in the words of Victor Hugo, "He who is a legend in his own time, is ruled by that legend. It may begin in absolute innocence.

But, to cover up flaws and maintain the myth of Divine Power one has to employ desperate measures."

Pastor's frequent moves of desperation, a growing concern with my influence and emerging freedom, and uneasiness with the new worship style converged to create public blow-ups. I was his whipping boy and public berating of me in staff meetings became a frequent occurrence.

I was provided a respite. Our missions pastor had been after me to take a trip to a country in Central Asia called Kyrgyzstan. I had never heard of it, did not like to fly, and as I've told you before, I'm a homebody. But it seemed a good time to get out of Dodge.

As we cleared security at Heathrow in London for the second leg of our journey, there was a delay because even the seasoned British guard had never seen the FRU airport code for Bishkek, the capital city of Kyrgyzstan. Let's just say it is not a well-known mecca of tourism.

After twenty-eight hours of grueling travel, we stepped off the plane only to wearily hop into a dilapidated van with balding tires for another harrowing eight-hour drive. We finally arrived at Karakol, a town nestled in the Tian Shan Mountains. I was literally in the middle of nowhere. If you put a finger on the opposite side of the world from Nashville, it would be right around Kyrgyzstan.

It was in the middle of this deep fatigue and fear of an alien Muslim world that I experienced a moment of transcendence. My assignment during the trip was to present a lecture to young Muslim college students about art and free enterprise. All of the art in this third-world country was utilitarian. There were crude pictures of their homes called yurts, simple paintings of rugs with the Kyrgyz symbol, and wooden sketches of the Tian Shan Mountains. There was no concept of creating art simply for art's sake.

As my words channeled through a Kyrgyz interpreter, you could have heard a pin drop. The Muslim "college" classroom was far more primitive than the one-room schoolhouses of my Appalachian heritage. The desks were far too small for the students and the concrete room was freezing cold.

197

There was an overwhelming smell of body odor and looking out the smoky and broken panes of glass, I could see rivers of human excrement running down the streets. There are still moments when I catch a similar nuance of that unique smell and am instantly transported back to that impoverished country.

There were no computers or televisions. I learned later there was only one photocopier in the entire town and it was usually broken. I had never witnessed poverty at this level. The eyes of the older people were filled with hopelessness. Most were bleary from the effects of cheap Russian vodka.

But the students huddled in this dingy classroom had a glimmer of hope in their eyes. As I talked about the beauty and uniqueness of their flora and fauna and the architectural grandeur of the multi-colored Russian Orthodox cathedral in the center of their town, their faces filled with pride.

Walking out afterwards, trying to avoid the rivulets of human excrement, a male student ran after me calling, "Rhan-dee, Rhan-dee, Ostanovit. (Stop!) Ostanovit. (Stop!)" After apologizing for being so abrupt, he asked for a word with me through the interpreter. I said, "Of course."

He said, "My name is Rafael and may I please to ask, what is your dream? What is your dream, Rhan-dee?" I replied, "I'm living my dream, Rafael. I have traveled to your country to teach about art. I sing and paint. I'm an artist. I am living my dream. Now may I ask, what is *your* dream, Rafael?"

He promptly said, "Ahhhh, I dream to be a rapper like Ja Rule or to be a basketball player like Kobe."

My head started to spin. In all my life, there has never been a sentence that impacted me in that way.

I had landed in a country the world had forgotten, and if that wasn't enough, I had driven eight hours farther into the middle of nothingness, surrounded by a seemingly impenetrable mountain range. I was shivering from the cold with snow flying by in a street paved with mud. My shoes were caked with human feces (they smelled so bad I had to throw them away when I got home) and I was in a poverty-stricken town lined with drab and depressing

198

utilitarian communist-era buildings that were disintegrating.

We could not find a television in the town; the electricity almost never worked; and this Kyrgyz kid, *who had never been out of this town,* had just confidently told me the two most fervent dreams of his life. And they were both influenced by American entertainment—an industry that to this young man might as well have been millions of light-years away.

The arts had somehow provided hope in the middle of despair. If art could inspire the youth in this town, I was convinced it could reach anywhere on earth.

Several events foreshadowed my life-changing moment with Rafael. I had recently read Bob Briner's *Roaring Lambs,* which states that we must engage in the discourse of our culture. He challenged Christians to involve themselves in the culture-shaping arenas of art, entertainment, the media, and education.

I heard Barry Landis, former President of Word Records, speak at Vanderbilt University in Nashville, about developing what he called "Artist Training Centers" to mentor and encourage young creatives.

And I had read *Diffusions of Innovations* by Everett Rogers, which explains how new ideas spread via communication channels over time. But such innovations are initially perceived as uncertain and even risky.

He suggests seeking out others of one's tribe who have already adopted the new idea. Thus the diffusion process consists of a few people who first adopt an innovation, then spread the word among their circle of acquaintances—a process which typically takes months or years.

To me, this diffusion of the arts could most effectively be accomplished by an existing institution like the church. Since arriving at Church #5, I had felt that if any church could influence the arts in a positive way, it would be this one. We were in a burgeoning cultural center, our philosophy had attracted a plethora of artists and creatives, and we were ideally situated in the epicenter of it all.

Sadly, soon after our departure, the American college student who had served as our guide was brutally attacked

199

in Karakol and left for dead. The organization that brought us there felt it was Muslim radicals who had been forced north to the Kyrgyzstan mountains from Afghanistan by our Armed Forces. All Americans were advised to leave the town. I was never able to communicate with Rafael again.

Immediately upon arriving back home, I began to prepare a plan for implementing an Artist Training Center at our church. At the next executive staff meeting, I asked permission to interview celebrities, recording artists, and professionals in the music industry about feasibility of what I called an ATC.

I was begrudgingly granted time each Thursday for a period of six months to conduct these interviews. With each conversation, my excitement grew. But as my enthusiasm was building, I could sense trepidation in the pastor and executive pastor—the two guys who were my supervisors.

A few weeks later, Pastor asked me to lunch. Just before we got out of the car, in front of his office, he said, "Randy, you know you can't build a church on artists. It just isn't possible. We are trying to build a viable church here." I was stunned. I stammered, "Then why would you even have me on staff? For God's sake, my title is 'Pastor of Arts.' If we can't build a church on artists, what am I supposed to do?"

There was a typical extended silence and so I numbly got out of the car. I managed to get through the day and wearily drove home where I fell into my favorite chair and began to weep.

I was surrounded by the crowd of people I had seen die the previous years: my voice teacher while directing *Messiah*; Mr. Rosser on stage; Jim, the choir member who died in terror; Alayna who had been killed at youth group; the chairman of the deacons lying on the emergency room table—and they were all singing a funeral dirge for my dreams.

A chilling and heavy tiredness settled over my body like a frozen winter. Forty-seven years of legalism, rules, and regulations. Twenty-five years of doing good deeds and ministering to others. Twenty-five years of attending to everyone's soul but my own. All I could do was cry.

Uncontrollably. The hours upon days upon years of meetings, ministry, and doing had caught up with me. My soul had finally withered away.

Through my tears, I told my wife I was not going back to work. She replied, "Oh yes, you are. You've just got to be a man and face up to all of this." She suggested seeing a counselor.

I did indeed put my "big boy pants" back on and return to work. But it was never the same.

Around that time, our church hired a famous high-priced consultant to evaluate our present situation and offer recommendations for the future. He spent several months interviewing everyone from the custodians, volunteers, randomly selected members, teachers, every staff member, and even people who had left the church. The interviews were held in complete confidence and the probing questions were intense.

The process culminated with a two-day executive staff retreat with the consultant at a conference hotel near Atlanta. After a preliminary recap of the entire process, he unveiled the recommendations he felt would propel us into a promising future.

To my complete surprise, the very first item was the idea of an Artist Training Center. Silence greeted his opening proposition and I did not speak since everyone knew it was my idea. So he awkwardly went on to the second—a unique look at small group Bible study. This elicited the expected conversation, as did all the subsequent proposals.

At the next meeting the consultant asked why we had been unresponsive to the first recommendation for the Artist Training Center, saying he had purposely put them in order of priority. Silence again permeated the room until finally the executive pastor said, "I suppose, to put it crudely, we don't see how this Artist Training Center will put butts in the pews."

The consultant skillfully defended his number-one suggestion but the response was tepid at best. At the next break, he privately asked if I would be willing to speak to the proposal. He felt my research and passion for the idea might carry some weight with my colleagues. I hesitantly agreed.

As I began speaking, I intuitively realized the next few minutes could change the course of my career. I went all in. For over an hour, I passionately told the story of Rafael in Kyrgyzstan, about the influence of Bob Briner's book *Roaring Lambs*, and about the concept of a tribe diffusing ideas. When I finally sat down, I was spent.

The executive pastor said, "Randy, you're pretty committed to this idea. What are you going to do if we decide not to implement it?" After thinking a moment, I replied, "I guess we'll have to wait and see, won't we?"

The retreat only added to my growing disillusionment with the ministry, and the consultant's number-one recommendation (the Artist Training Center) was never mentioned again as part of the church.

When I signed my contract back in 2000, part of the agreement was a month-long Sabbatical after five years of service. It was now late 2005 and it felt like an opportune time. No staff member had ever taken a Sabbatical and even though Pastor had been privy to the initial negotiation, he suddenly wasn't happy about the idea.

Long ago he had arranged to have a month off each summer for study leave, but no other staff member had ever asked for extended time off. Pastor's "study leave" was a point of contention with the staff because the only tangible evidence from his annual month away was a lower golf handicap. The creative team's plea for his time away to be used for planning sermons six months in advance went unheeded.

I suppose he thought I would utilize my time in much the same way he did—so he stonewalled the leave request. But the agreement was in writing and on file, and I took my case to the personnel team. They not only allowed me to take the month-long Sabbatical but let me add my four weeks of vacation to the time as well.

For the first time since I was twelve years old, I was to have two months off from work to do with as I wished. It was an extravagant gift from heaven. I did not take it lightly.

A friend of mine let me use his isolated log cabin deep in the Colorado Rockies. I loaded up my army green Jeep Willys with books, journals, and art supplies and began the two-day journey out West. My wife was consumed with her job so we planned for her to come out a couple of times for a week or so as her responsibilities allowed. By this time, the girls had jobs and limited vacation time.

My life coach suggested I do a tech fast, so immediately upon arrival I turned off all the clocks and the television. There was no Internet or cell service available; so to communicate with the outside world, each week I would drive to the nearby town about ten miles away.

At first the quiet and solitude were intensely frightening; the silence was so loud you could hear it. But after two or three days I began to settle into it. I climbed a few fourteeners (fourteen-thousand-foot mountains) to get the testosterone out of my system and then began to do the real work of my Sabbatical—something I knew little about —resting, and being, and getting to know myself. That task was much harder than I could have ever dreamed. There is a reason we work so hard and run from ourselves: we don't care to face the truth.

Several things spoke deeply to me. Books that would expectedly move me in the real world became earthshaking in solitude. Passages such as:

> We feel important because someone considers us indispensable. In short, we are worthwhile because we have successes. And the more we allow our accomplishments—the results of our actions—to become the criteria of our self-esteem, the more we are going to walk on our mental and spiritual toes, never sure if we will be able to live up to the expectations which we created by our last successes. In many people's lives, there is a nearly diabolic chain in which their anxieties grow according to their successes. This dark power has

203

driven many of the greatest artists into self-destruction.[4]

My life coach had also challenged me to chronologically review my life journals and look for patterns and "eureka" moments. I have not been the best at daily journaling, but I did have a fairly consistent and honest record of my life scrawled down into nine separate binders. Several discoveries came from this invaluable time.

First, I had forgotten much of the magic and wonder of my life. Tears flowed freely as I read handwritten accounts of my two daughter's first steps and first words and moments from their birthdays and school. There were honest times of questioning God and a sincerity and innocence in the early years of ministry that humbled me.

Second, from my teens until present day, there were few gaping holes in my thoughts; but one stood out. As I mentioned earlier, there was not a single entry during the seven years spent at Church #4. Every fiber of my being had been consumed pleasing and ministering to others. There had been no time for anything else—even myself.

Third, the valuable time spent journaling throughout life provides invaluable gifts later in life. At times, it seemed the random insights and musings were from a stranger—but Miss Sorrells' influence on my standard cursive handwriting was unmistakable. I was being introduced to myself for the first time in my life. And it was a bittersweet time—like a sunset—a happy sadness.

Fourth, I realized my most fulfilling times throughout the years had been when I was mentoring and encouraging others one-on-one or in small groups like my *re:create Conference*. Those times provided more fulfillment than serving at mega-churches, more than singing for tens of thousands, more than rubbing shoulders with celebrities, and more than any of my entrepreneurial successes.

---

[4] Henri Nouwen, *Out of Solitude: Three Meditations on the Christian Life,* First Meditation, 2004.

During the last two weeks of that fateful time, I decided to resign from Church #5. After much conversation, my wife concurred.

But when I returned to the real world, I chickened out. I was accustomed to a regular paycheck. I really didn't know how to proceed with the Artist Training Center, and to be candid, I was afraid of the unknown. So I kept putting it off. Besides, who the hell quits in his prime?

Back in the office, Pastor's irritation was disappearing, and I was glad, but I knew him well enough to know that it was bubbling around under a thin surface. The executive pastor, long Pastor's best friend, sensed a war was in the offing.

I became increasingly intolerant of Pastor's lack of civility toward other staff members. In general, we were growing apart, and our friendship was lost.

One morning a youth pastor I really liked showed up unexpectedly at my office. He proceeded to tell me he was resigning to try his hand at acting in Los Angeles. He had also been influenced by the *Roaring Lambs* movement.

As I congratulated him and told him how proud I was of him, I asked if he had told Pastor yet. He just laughed and said, "I've been here for three years and not once has he darkened the door of my office. I don't even know him. You have encouraged me so I thought you should be the executive team member to know. I'm gone."

A few months later, the executive pastor called and requested a breakfast appointment. He cut to the chase and said, "I have some things to say that you're not going to like. I'm requiring every pastor to have office hours, you included. We need to be more like a team, and if one of us isn't there, everyone knows it."

I replied, "You don't need me to twiddle my thumbs at a desk all day. Encouraging and mentoring my staff, the creative team, and the artists and musicians is what I do best. You're right, I don't like it."

He had more to say but at that moment, I knew I was done. No need to offer an explanation, no point in engaging in further discussion, and certainly no call for sentiment or nostalgia.

I stopped him and said, "I'm through. I resign. You can have a two-weeks notice, or if you like I'll stay on a while longer and mentor my assistant." He seemed stunned but ever the professional he replied, "Okay, I'll talk to Pastor. Two weeks—or longer if we like."

We shook hands and I left. And just that fast, my twenty-nine years as a minister of music and arts came to an end.

I drove to a local park and sat in the grass under an ancient oak tree and watched people stroll by. The lush beauty of Tennessee never ceases to send a shiver up my spine. The pungent smell of a wild onion nearby reminded me of the tiny pleasures I had missed in the past three decades.

As I sat there, I thought back to a late afternoon a few months ago. We live in the Central Time Zone (in the mountains old-timers called it "slow time") and it was already dark. I was at church and the bluish glow of a computer screen burned through Pastor's study window.

I had just finished a late rehearsal and it was past dinnertime. In happier years, he would have jumped at an invitation from me to grab a bite at his favorite restaurant just a minute down the road. A moment of empathic softness engulfed me and I pulled my Jeep into a parking spot and slipped in the back door.

I was one of only three or four people to possess a key to his private entrance. A long hallway first led to an entry room and then to a small snack room. There was a door for each room providing layers of privacy, but for some reason they were both open. He didn't hear me sidle in.

He was intently staring at the computer screen, unaware that anyone was around. It was facing me so I could see it as well. For a brief second, I breathed a prayer that he was looking at some guilty pleasure. Anything that would prove he still had a spark of life or human passion. But it was worse.

The screen was filled with his inbox. It was empty. And as I stood there I heard the ding of an incoming email. He anxiously opened it, read it, assigned it to some digital portion of hell, and then resumed his vigil. In a moment, another ding, another deletion. Thinking he was waiting for an emergency email, it suddenly occurred to me—this is what he did every night.

By his own admission, he had sacrificed the quality of his home life for the "demands" of the ministry. And his girls sure had no hesitation in bitterly proclaiming that to anybody who would listen.

He had nowhere to go. And no one to be with. His wife had once said publicly that he eventually pushes away all his closest friends.

Musing under that tree in the park, I didn't feel pushed away; on the contrary, I felt a freedom like nothing I had ever experienced.

# PART III
# THE RENAISSANCE YEARS

# CHAPTER 17

# HOME SWEET HOME

On the first day of June 2006, I marched out to my Jeep Wrangler, put the top down, and pulled away from the church office for the last time. I kicked it into second gear, popped the clutch, and got a little rubber just for the heck of it. Hitting fourth gear, the warm wind of freedom blew the few curls I had left into a tangled mess.

By the time I shoved it into sixth gear, I was blaring at the top of my lungs the song I had carefully chosen for this moment: "Nah, nah nah, NAH—nah nah, NAH, nah nah, nah . . . " It was the theme song of *Rocky*. I was flyin' high.

211

Speeding off into the perfect Tennessee spring day, I headed home. Or at least to where I had always thought was home.

After endless days alone in a dream house that was now too big for *my* life, my two girls gone chasing their dreams, and my wife finally having the chance to live her own, I realized I had forgotten where I came from. A sense of vertigo gripped my being.

I had no idea where home was anymore. I felt lost and confused. My life-long Faustian pact with the ministry had cost my inner consciousness.

Alone with my true self and nothing to do for the first time in my life, I hated the emptiness within. I was beginning to grasp the toll the ministry had taken. It had enriched and enlivened my life beyond all imagination, but it had also left me asking, "Who am I?" How much of what I did in pushing the limits of worship styles and exploring uncharted territory was a compensation for my dad's unlived life? How much of this life was truly mine, and not some religious agenda derived from him? Was it fear that had kept me in the ministry so long?

When I was young, I fantasized that I could change the world; but now I felt like nothing more than a slave to my desperate need for approval. Ah, how ignorant we are of ourselves.

Once I realized I could never bring myself to return to the church, I became angry—angry that I'd been used, angry that no one missed me, and angry at myself for having sacrificed so much for people who had so little appreciation for what I'd given up.

The thing I longed for most was someone who understood this existential angst. Someone who would entertain my probing questions. A soul mate who felt the same way I did. I needed a sympathetic ear.

It hurt so desperately that the people closest to me didn't understand my cries for help. I had an ever-widening hole in my heart and the pain alienated me from those I loved most. My life seemed not to matter to anyone.

I felt like a journal that had been torn into a thousand pieces and thrown into the ether. The lyrics to the song "Dust in the Wind" replaced the theme song from *Rocky*.

"Like a drop of water in an endless sea, all we do, crumbles to the ground, though we refuse to see." [5]

It was into this vortex of despair I stumbled and fell.

It is a universal truth in spiritual literature that in order to truly succeed in life, we must fail at something. But all my life I'd had—what my type-A friend who worked in the commodities pit in Chicago called—"a golden horseshoe shoved up my ass." I had the Midas touch. I could do no wrong.

I had married my childhood sweetheart, escaped the poverty of the Appalachians, had two beautiful girls, climbed to the pinnacle of success in my vocation, started a company in my garage and sold it at the height of the Nasdaq boom, and was able to retire at the zenith of my career at the preposterous age of forty-seven.

I was a social media darling, lived in an affluent utopian neighborhood with the leaders and influencers of Christendom, my events for the religious glitterati were not to be missed, and I was touted as a renaissance man.

I had never experienced a situation in life that did not eventually turn out golden. It was the American dream. A rags-to-riches story.

But in the middle of all this, I was experiencing a deep hunger for wholeness. I longed for a place where my consciousness and reason—which had been in a constant struggle all my life—were at peace with one another. I was homesick for something "real."

My wife in her busyness sensed something was wrong and urged me to paint more often. It was obvious my times with watercolor were healthy for me. Urging me to get out into nature, she encouraged me to try painting *plein air*. She also suggested I call long-time friends of ours and ask if I could hike and explore their sprawling farm for subject matter.

A few days later as I drove my Jeep crammed with art supplies up the long winding driveway, my consciousness thrilled with anticipation—but as I topped the driveway and saw my hostess sitting on the front steps with a huge

---

[5] Kansas, "Dust in the Wind." Words by Kerry Livgren, 1977.

smile, I was suddenly apprehensive. I felt an intuitive shiver of adrenaline and foreboding and for a moment considered waving and turning the Jeep around and leaving. But I didn't.

The lady was ten years my junior and married with young children. She was an active volunteer at church and we had crossed paths many times, but I had never been to their home. As she approached the Jeep, she invited me to take a look inside to say hello to her kids. I asked about her husband and she casually told me he was away (as usual, she added) on a business trip.

I was introduced to the children, and after a few short moments said, "Well, I better get to it." As we walked out, she offered to show me around the property, saying she had identified a few places that may be ideal spots for painting.

As she pulled on her hiking boots, it struck me how attractive she was. Around the church she had always seemed gangly, gracious, and witty, but seeing her in this setting made things different somehow.

She was clad in faded jeans and an old flannel shirt; her swinging long hair was straight in the style of the seventies. Her earthy manner was a studied contrast to my experience of females. Drawing closer to grab my backpack, she smelled of white cotton, reminiscent of the fresh spring day.

As she guided me down a picturesque wooded trail, my head swirled and I couldn't catch my breath. As we reached a creek bank, she turned with a half-smile and looked me straight in the eyes. Her stare was unflinching and searching. I saw the reflection of my soul.

As I struggled to breathe, she said, "Are you okay?" I stammered, "Yes." But she knew I wasn't. It was a sensual moment of vulnerability, unlike anything I had experienced in my life. She had stolen my heart with that one look.

You should know that I went to my marriage bed a virgin and had never once breached my vow of monogamy. Not that I hadn't had opportunities. When you are a young religious celebrity, a musician, and on stage in front of thousands, you are always a target. But despite several advances by very attractive women over the years, I had never given infidelity a second thought. It was almost as if God had always guarded my heart. But for reasons I'm still not clear about, there was no defender that day.

I shook my head to clear the dizziness. She gently suggested I sit on a nearby fallen log for a moment and catch my breath. I sunk down wearily into the sponginess of the thick moss, and for some reason I began to talk.

And she listened. When I would finally stop for a moment to take a breath, her insightful responses told me that she understood what I was saying. Her intense listening was god-like and intoxicating. She heard me. She really heard me.

Nothing physical happened that day, but an intimacy and an emotional bond was forged that was more powerful than any sexual experience I had ever known. We both had a deep and desperate loneliness that comes when you find yourself confronting mortality and the meaning of life—but all your friends and family are still in the throes of immortality and achieving success.

We talked Rand, Dostoevsky, O'Donohue, Dante, and Shakespeare. We asked each other existential questions without judgment or fear. Questions like, "Why can't we define ourselves by our own standards, rather than an external moral code? Do we really believe each person has complete freedom of choice?" We discussed objectivism, rationalism, and theism.

I had never met a person who possessed the words to articulate and respond intelligently to my deepest and most penetrating questions about God, religion, life, and meaning. So I suppose it was inevitable we would eventually discuss love.

We were both very fragile. My peers, friends, and family did not understand—and if they were truthful, were probably embarrassed by—my counter-cultural decision to quit work at age forty-seven. Many of my guy friends jokingly called me a "kept man." Heck, I was struggling to understand why I had taken this new path myself.

She was a young lady in her intellectual and sexual prime who felt trapped by her children (even though she loved them dearly) and her responsibilities as a mom. Her husband was a very successful businessman and was often away. Both our spouses were too busy to listen responsively and the structure of our lives provided little, if any, accountability.

It took six months of constant companionship before we consummated our relationship. We didn't want the sexual tension to get in the way of this beautiful and unprecedented friendship. But the "soulish knowing" each of us was experiencing was too powerful. We succumbed. The desire overrode the guilt and common sense, and for two months we embarked on what can only be described as a torrid affair.

It was like something you see in the movies or read about in fairy tales. Except this was real life. And real people with real emotions with real moral convictions were involved.

I have always sucked at covering things up. I'm a "what you see is what you get" kinda guy. I most identify with King David in the Bible. And so the guilt consumed me. I felt I was betraying my wife, her husband, our children, and our marriage covenants. Oh yeah, and I had never quite gotten the New Testament grace thing, so I kept expecting God to mete out Old Testament fire and brimstone.

Without getting caught and without being found out, I did what I thought was the right thing at the time and followed the Biblical process of confession to my wife and asked forgiveness. She granted it, but her own life and religious experiences created a struggle with reconciliation.

Because there were young children involved, all parties kept the matter private. In an unbelievable act of forgiveness, my friend's husband met with me a few months later and forgave me. He told me they were in counseling and that he realized his need to be a better husband. He went on to say he had asked what she missed most about me, and she replied, "The friendship. I feel I've lost a very dear friend."

My wife and I also went to my life coach from Church #5, but we did not realize he was unlicensed as a marriage counselor.

216

My psychologist in later life—who holds a PhD in marriage and family therapy—upon hearing a recounting of our analysis, said the well-meaning but untrained church counselor had done "surgery" on our marriage, but did not have the skills to do "chemotherapy."

About a year after I had confessed my indiscretion, I received a call from my former pastor at Church #5. He asked for a coffee appointment. It was an unusual request, since I had heard nothing from him—nothing—since I had resigned. It had been almost two years since we had talked.

In fact, except for two close friends on the arts staff, not one person from Church #5 had ever called me since the day I resigned.

I was glad Pastor called; I desperately missed the camaraderie of the staff and I hoped he was missing me too. But as I approached the table I could see a familiar sight—he was shaking with anger. He had just learned about the affair. The way he found out is layered with irony.

Just before I decided to confess, I had suggested that my paramour see one of the pastor's wives at Church #5 for counseling about the affair. She had not decided to do so until recently; but as it so often goes in a church, after a while the confidante told her husband, who felt bound by "loyalty" to tell Pastor.

He began to berate me and seething, he told me he regretted ever calling me to his church. I felt the chill of his shame permeate my body.

I stood up trembling with hurt and somehow found the courage to reply, "I'm not your boy any longer. This happened long after I left *your* church. It is none of your business. I've asked forgiveness from all the affected parties and have been granted it." With each word I felt a growing sense of anger, "I should bash your face in right now!" I added some choice four-letter words and walked out. I've never seen the man again but another part of me died that day, just as my soul had finally started to recover a bit.

My wife and I tried to restore the broken trust, but the next five years were tenuous at best. Rather than helping, the religious-tinged counseling and my growing

217

disillusionment with God made things worse. We only grew apart.

We tried moving to the main street of our historic downtown, hoping a change of scenery would do us good. But the situation only worsened. I began to drink more often.

I also wrestled with existential longings and questions by writing my first book, *Sex, Lies & Religion*. Our counselor suggested I paint the angst I was feeling while writing the book and my watercolors grew increasingly sensual. None of this was received well by my family and friends. I felt so alone.

Our new house sat between two fire halls and beside a newly opened and extravagant police station; so the wailing of the sirens and the growing noise pollution never seemed to stop. The incessant sirens that blared and interrupted the peaceful downtown setting began to create an increasing distress and anger in me.

I was now drinking even more heavily, smoking cigars (something I had never done), and was increasingly disillusioned by the constant posing and posturing of the community we had developed in our "Christian" downtown. In many ways, the society of our hyper-religious and affluent town reminded me of a dysfunctional church.

When I would look at those people, I would say to myself, "If that's success, I don't know that I want to be successful. If heaven looks like this town, I don't want to go there."

All this time, I struggled to produce my flourishing *re:create Conference* each year and when I would present my keynote speech, I would be candid and honest about my struggles without betraying confidences by being too forthcoming—but felt little empathy from the gathering.

It was into this climate that Gina Kremkau, a close friend of the family (over twenty years) moved from Atlanta into one of our investment properties—a townhouse apartment. She had recently gone through a divorce after thirty-five years of fidelity and marriage and was trying to get a new start.

218

She had always been like a sister to me. We had a strictly platonic relationship that consisted of things like racing each other down the mountains on ski trips. She also had been chairman of the personnel team that hired me at Church #4.

She smoked cigars, drank cocktails, loved my book, and savored my sensual paintings. And she listened to me with an even deeper responsiveness (if that is possible) than my previous confidante.

My addiction to approval, combined with her vibrant love for life, made me relish every moment with her. We filled each other's emptiness.

And so I failed to keep my marriage vows for the second time in my life. This affair lasted about two months before one evening, after too much to drink, I was found out. Getting caught was still a better fate than the overwhelming guilt.

Again I begged for forgiveness, but this time my marriage of thirty-two years was over. My wife had had enough.

There are fewer things I regret more than the way I handled those six years after I stepped off stage and left the ministry; and there are no feelings from that time that compare with the sadness I feel over the pain I caused my family (especially my wife and two daughters) and friends and those who trusted me as their leader at *re:create*.

Except for a few of my closest friends, I was ostracized by the Christian community. I had sinned—and that made me bad for business. My expansive social networks dried up overnight and people and sponsors began to pull out of my conference and my life. It was as though I did not exist. For months on end, I would not receive one email or call.

Nashville is a very small town, and our suburb even smaller. So I fled in shame.

I had recently met new friends in Austin, Texas, who told me it was a place where many people come for a new start and that I would find it much more accepting than the Bible Belt. I instinctively knew I needed grace if I were to survive. The confusion over the past six years was overwhelming.

219

I also knew I would not survive alone. The depression and pain had made me suicidal (an emotion I had never experienced before) and so I asked Gina to accompany me to a city in which neither of us had ever remotely considered living.

It was late summer of 2011, and the first one hundred days we lived there it was over a hundred degrees Fahrenheit. It was an apt metaphor for the hell I was experiencing.

Just before Christmas I traveled back to Nashville once more in a guilt-filled attempt to reconcile with my wife. Gina remained in Austin crushed and confused. I was hurting everyone I cared most about.

My attempt was rebuffed and I wearily returned home. It was a few days before the dawning of 2012, and somehow with the help of a new psychologist, I resolved to use the New Year as impetus to begin rebuilding my life from the ashes.

When I had first arrived in Austin in September, Ramy, a new friend who was a pastor at Gateway Church (known for their acceptance of imperfect people) recommended I grab coffee with Ted Beasley who had co-founded the church, a man he highly respected and assured me was safe. For some inexplicable reason, I went. That day turned out to be another one of those rare appointments with destiny that change everything.

As the bitter aroma of Cortados permeated the vibey downtown coffee shop on Congress Avenue, this no-nonsense but very articulate and empathic guy (who ironically had formerly been a teaching pastor with Hybels at Willow Creek) listened patiently to my story. I held nothing back. I had nothing to lose. It was the cold, unadulterated truth. I told him everything but my underwear size. And would have told him that if he had asked.

He suggested I see a psychologist friend of his—saying I would never be able to get in on my own—but he would try to call in a favor. He told me his friend specialized in helping people get off stage and get healthy.

He warned me not to see any other therapist in Austin, especially not church counselors. He looked me straight in

220

the eyes and said, "Randy, I believe you've never properly grieved the loss of your ministry." I digested that statement for a few moments and then agreed to see his psychologist friend.

For the next two years, each week I poured my heart out to this highly trained and empathic doctor. I was soon convinced the main reason I had "randomly" moved to Austin was to receive this therapy and healing. Good things can come out of bad decisions.

My confusion and disappointment at the loss of my old groups, friendships, and social networks was far outdistanced by a new ability to appreciate simplicity. My circle of real confidants and truly close friends had grown much smaller, but had become much more intimate. For the first time in my life, I was living free and clear with those who truly mattered. That freedom was exhilarating.

A year after my divorce was final, and with the professional guidance and blessing of my psychologist, I asked Gina to marry me. More than my lover and friend, she is my muse. However, I have learned that she is not responsible to be my soul mate. Nor is anyone else. After a lifetime of searching in vain for a soul mate, I've finally realized that responsibility is mine alone.

Loving and caring for my soul is not indulgent service to my ego, rather it is how I believe God chooses to live through me. Our souls are what *we* are called to bring into this world—to contribute to our society, our families, and to share with others.

Another year passed, and with the advice and blessing of my therapist, Gina and I felt it was important to return home. Because I am a Southerner. True I left the mountains and traveled the far corners of the world for a while. But I am a still a Southerner. Always have been. Always will be.

The previous six years had been the worst possible years of my life. My marriage of thirty-two years was ruined, my children are deeply hurt, I have a grandson I've yet to meet, and I almost lost my business.

It doesn't make a bit of sense, but it is the greatest thing that ever happened to me—that I lost everything. It took something that drastic to wound my soul and bring me back home. To put it rather crudely, the "golden horseshoe" had to be ripped out because somehow it had reached up my ass and attached itself to my soul. In the words of Julian of Norwich, "God sees our wounds, and sees them not as scars but as honors. . . . For he holds sin as a sorrow and pain to his lovers. He does not blame us for them."[6]

In Biblical terms, despite his sins of adultery and murder—David was chosen to bear the lineage of Jesus Christ himself. If we really believe this is true, what seems the end becomes the beginning.

I once heard someone say that everyone has two lives: the one we live and the one yet unlived.

I also learned from the works of Dr. James Masterson that it is the knowledge of our real self that enables us to experiment in work, as in love, to find and achieve the sense of personal meaning essential for a fulfilling life.

One of the great revelations of my life is coming to full consciousness (to wholeness) by facing my contradictions, making friends with my mistakes and failings, and realizing that every one else has them too. This has tempered my need for approval and the unreasonable expectations I've had for myself, my family, and my friends.

Instead of approaching each relationship expecting 100 percent—but being bitterly disappointed by getting only getting 50 percent—I'm learning to come to each relationship expecting zero and being pleasantly surprised when I receive anything at all.

Even as I write the words of this memoir, I'm an aggregation of the various persons (redneck and renaissance; pastor and artist) I have been in the past. And as I begin this unlived life—this second half of life—I'm learning to relate and reconcile them all to each other to form a whole and vibrant story.

---

[6] Julian of Norwich, *Revelations of Divine Love,* Chapter 39, Showing 13.

In the words of Saint Symeon the younger, "For the One who has become many, remains the One undivided, but each part is all of Christ." [7]

What I am today is the product of the ever-changing roles, behaviors, and circumstances that make this book come to life. They fitted me then, and when viewed through the wisdom of a wounded soul, they still fit today.

May we realize that losing, failing, falling, sin,
and the suffering that comes with these
experiences—
all of this is a necessary and even good part
of our human journey.
May we realize we grow spiritually much more
by doing it wrong than by doing it right.
May we realize that home is both the beginning
and the end.
May we realize that home is but an inner
compass
and a North Star.
May we realize that home is but a metaphor for
our soul.
May death not pose a threat,
because we have lived with fullness
both halves of our lives.

---

[7] Translated by Dom Ansgar Nelson, O.S.B. in *The Soul Afire* (New York: Pantheon Books, 1944) p. 303.

For bonus photos, extras, deluxe edition information, and much more, visit and subscribe to email updates at the official website:

http://renaissanceredneck.com

Randy would be honored if you would write a review at the book's Amazon page.

Also, please take a moment and share this book with your friends on your favorite social network.

# THANKS

To **Alice Sullivan**, my editor, whose tireless hours, sense of humor, and creative expertise made these redneck words, colloquialisms, and stories blend into a compelling and beautiful work of renaissance art.

To **Margaret Becker**, **Paulette Wooten**, and **The Nashville Treehouse Recording Studio** for creating a masterful audiobook and for taking my tired and aching voice and making it rich and resonant.

CPSIA information can be obtained at www.ICGtesting.com
Printed in the USA
BVOW09s0947120214

344698BV00002B/60/P